971
FE   Ferguson, Linda

          Canada

DATE			
APR 2 1 1980 OC 26 '99			
APR 2 2 1980			
MAY 7 1980			
DEC 1 1980			
NO 3 '86			
MR31 '87			
FE 1 7 '89			
AP 1 6 '91			
DE 26 '91			
JAN 1 9 95			
JUN 2 5 97			

CANADA

CHARLES SCRIBNER'S SONS
NEW YORK

LINDA FERGUSON

CANADA

Copyright © 1979 Linda W. Ferguson

Library of Congress Cataloging in Publication Data
Ferguson, Linda.
Canada.
Bibliography: p.
Includes index.
SUMMARY: Surveys the history of Canada from the
earliest Asian civilizations to today.
1. Canada—History—Juvenile literature.
2. Indians of North America—Canada—History—Juvenile
literature. [1. Canada—History.   2. Indians of North
America—Canada—History.   3. Eskimos—Canada—History]
I. Title.
F1026.F46   971   79-15871
ISBN 0-684-16080-3

1 3 5 7 9 11 13 15 17 19 V/C 20 18 16 14 12 10 8 6 4 2

To A. B. Ferguson

ACKNOWLEDGMENTS

This book owes its existence to contributions from a number of people—in particular Corinne Goudie of the Canadian Consulate General in San Francisco, whose knowledge of Canadian reference material, periodicals, literature, art, and current events was seemingly inexhaustible, and who was immeasurably helpful and generous over the long haul; also Tom Johnson of the National Film Board of Canada, who made it possible for me to screen many hours of NFB film; also Rita Fink, who edited, researched, typed, translated, and nurtured.

Author E. G. Valens encouraged the manuscript in its early stages; David Ferretta helped correct galleys; Leslie Arnold encouraged me and helped with research; and a superb editor, Jonathan Sharp of Chandler and Sharp, read the final manuscript.

Francois Beaulne, formerly of the San Francisco consulate, offered invaluable insights into current Canadian politics, and Patricia Foland transformed a terrible jumble, amid difficult circumstances, into a perfectly typed final manuscript.

CONTENTS

CANADA

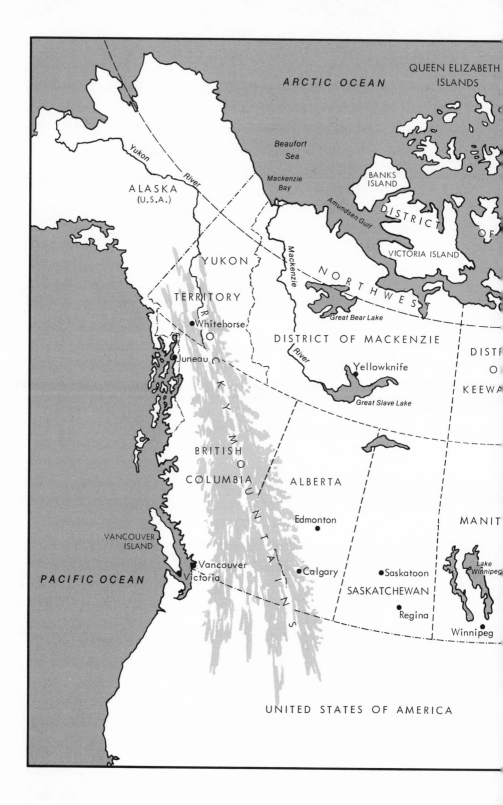

UNDER A BIG SKY

ONE

Summer is brief in the Canadian Arctic. Temperatures often do not rise above freezing. And even the sun that never sets in midsummer cannot melt the solid ice. The northernmost bays remain frozen or blocked by floes all year. The core ice pack of the North Pole has not thawed for millions of years.

Unlike the South Pole, the North Pole has no underlying land, just vast stretches of age-old ice. Land begins almost 500 miles south of the North Pole, with a group of Canadian islands called the Arctic Archipelago. As winter sets in, this world seems barren, empty. Even the snow is swept from the ice by the polar easterlies, and most of the day is dark, the sun only a faint glow on the horizon. It is a world of ice and night.

Yet the Arctic is not really bleak. The magnetic North Pole attracts solar particles, creating the spectacular Aurora Borealis which lights the Arctic night. Although the easterly winds sweep the ice, they are less bitter, less piercing than the winds farther south. Although it snows heavily, often less snow falls than in Chicago. Although it is cold, the temperature is often higher than in Montana. And although everything seems still and lifeless, many Arctic animals remain to struggle for survival throughout the long winter.

Large mammals, such as seal, walrus, and polar bear, live on the edge of the ice pack. They are specially equipped to face the cold sea by thick layers of fat under their skin, and to walk on slippery ice by specially designed paws or flippers. They live in the borderland between ice and water, at the precise point where water freezes. To sleep and breed, they need solid ice. To eat and travel, they need water. As the massive ice pack freezes southward in winter, the seal and walrus follow the water-ice edge for fish. And the polar bear follows the seal.

The polar is the largest, fiercest, and most carnivorous of bears. Aside from the human hunter, unstable ice is its only enemy; it is wary of being crushed by crashing floes or trapped beneath floating ice. In a world where most animals group together in order to survive, this creature often lives alone.

The exception is the female with her two cubs, who remain with her for a year or longer. She conceives in the spring, and by late fall when the ice pack freezes southward, she is torn between the gnaw of hunger and the lull of sleep. She needs to eat as much as possible before hibernation. Once she has fed, it is sleep that wins.

She walks inland, away from the treacherous ice. At last she finds a large hummock of snow in the lee of a hill. She hollows out the snow and curls into it, soon settling into a fitful winter sleep. Here in midwinter, in the dead of winter when ice is most packed and stable, two cubs will be born.

Overhead the Aurora Borealis fills the sky with trembling greens and yellows, and the polar easterlies sweep over the hill where the bear sleeps, lifting feathers of snow in the long night. The winds blow off the mountainsides of the eastern Arctic, puff across the ice-covered sea, then curve inland, where the flat terrain offers little obstruction.

South of the ice cap lies Barren Ground tundra, treeless plains and meadows of frozen land called permafrost. Though the surface may thaw slightly in summer, the permafrost goes down hundreds of feet. The ground is so moist that, when it does thaw, many sections become spongy and dotted with bog—or muskeg, as it is called in Canada.

Yet even this Barren Ground is filled with life. In summer, flowers and short grasses grow. There is a great deal of lichen, which is part fungus and part alga. Lichen and moss support herds of caribou and muskox. Farther south specialized plants, particularly creepers, grow in abundance. Still farther, dwarf trees dot the plains.

Some of the plants are almost in bud when winter comes. They wait in frozen sleep, ready to spring into bloom at the first hint of the short Arctic summer. Others die right down to the roots, which will have some protection in the winter ground. The lichen dries out and survives the harsh cold in a skeletal form. And as winter comes, the caribou migrate south to the woods.

The Barren Ground caribou, closely related to the reindeer, come to the tundra in the early spring, where they feed on lichen and other Arctic plants. In winter, they return to the Forest, where they live on twigs or scrape moss from snow-covered rocks. They make these migrations in large groups, sometimes numbering in the thousands. Their paths are long established and worn bare by countless migrations.

The caribou's only real protection from wolves and hunters is running; its large splayed hooves allow it to tread on snow and thawed permafrost without sinking. It avoids aggressive behavior even during rutting and will stand to fight only when desperately cornered. The caribou's attitude toward other animals seems to be a mixture of shyness and curiosity; although it breaks into a run at the first whisper of danger, it never goes far without stopping and looking back over its shoulder. Such gentleness seems not made for this harsh Arctic world, and in fact a lone caribou does not live very long.

Its survival depends on the group. Naturally sociable, the caribou divide into bands of individuals that all run at approximately the same speed. Wolves follow these bands, and the caribou that strays from the group falls prey to them.

Unlike the human hunter, wolves do not really deplete the caribou herd. The relationship between the two is symbiotic. Wolves usually attack the sick and old caribou, whose pace would slow down the group were they not culled. And in a land of scarce food, the group cannot afford to slow down as winter approaches. Their winter survival depends upon reaching the sheltering trees, where they can paw the snow for lichen and mosses, and nibble on twigs.

The first sign of woodland is the dwarf trees, no taller than shrubs, which hardly hint at the immense forest that lies beyond. This transition between tundra and forest continues for many miles, the trees gradually growing taller and closer. Then comes the Boreal Forest, hundreds of miles wide, stretching all the way across the continent. It comprises the largest single section of Canada, the greatest barely tapped resource of the nation.

The climate in the Forest is subarctic. The winters are sometimes harsher than in the Arctic, and permafrost extends over half of the area. Spruce is the dominant tree, although there is a good deal of fir, birch, aspen, and willow; near the thousands of lakes and muskeg swamps, tamarack grows. The landscape consists of trees, rock, and water in the summer, and of trees, snow, and ice in the winter. The countless lakes and waterways of this land are dotted with the dams and lodges of beaver.

Built of mud and sticks, the beaver lodge is stronger than many human-made houses. Since it can be entered only by water, from underneath, the beaver is safe from most predators. In winter, beavers stay indoors most of the time, drowsily tending to family business. The little ones live off twigs stored on the lodge floor, but their parents stop eating and live off their fat, waiting for spring to melt the ice.

Much of the Boreal Forest country lies on what is known as the Canadian Shield. Over a billion years ago, during the Pre-Cambrian age, a core of solid rock was created in the northern part of the North American continent. Composed of granites and gneisses, it covers 1,771,000 square miles, and rises above the surrounding plain anywhere between a few hundred and a few thousand feet. Roughly circular, it lies like a huge cored apple around Hudson Bay, completed in the north by mountainous Baffin Island. It is the oldest land in North America, its mountains worn to stumps, its surface scarred by the last great ice age. Because most of the topsoil was scraped from the Shield during the ice age, this great heartland may never have agricultural settlement. With its cold climate, sparse soil, thick forest, and treacherous muskeg, the Shield may never have much settlement of any type, except on its temperate southern fringes. And it covers about half of Canada.

It may seem that Canada is a tough, unyielding land of ice and forests, rock and muskeg. And so most of it is. But along its southern border is a strip averaging about 300 miles wide, running from coast to coast. Here the climate is more temperate, the soil more fertile, life more varied. In this warmer climate the variations in land from west to east become very important.

Most of western Canada, which includes British Columbia and the Yukon Territory, is high mountain country. These mountains leave only a tiny slice of lowland along the Coast. Alaska lies between the Yukon Territory and the ocean, and runs half the length of British Columbia. The Pacific Coast of Canada therefore comprises only the southern half of British Columbia.

The coastline is quite jagged. A submerged mountain chain offshore emerges as numerous islands, including the large Vancouver Island. On the continent itself, the Coast is indented with numerous fiords and small bays, cut off by high mountains from the rest of Canada.

Protected by mountains on the east and islands on the west, tempered by the sea, the Coast has a climate milder than anywhere else in Canada. In winter, rain is as likely as snow. Varieties of trees not found elsewhere in the country, such as the western red cedar and the sequoia, flourish in the mild, wet climate. The great Douglas fir grow to enormous heights.

Western Canada can claim not only the tallest trees and highest mountains in the country but also most of the largest rivers. The Mackenzie and Columbia flow from far inland, and the Yukon strikes diagonally across the Yukon Territory to the north. In the southeast are the rich lands of the Thompson and the Fraser River valleys.

It is late summer when the sockeye salmon leave their ocean feeding grounds and head for the Fraser River. They are in peak condition, as they must be to travel 700 miles upstream, against the swift muddy current, to their headwaters. They are returning to the place they were spawned five years before, in order to mate and to die. By the time they reach the spawning grounds, the males have grown long snouts with sharp teeth, and in both sexes the digestive organs have deteriorated. They die after spawning, leaving the eggs to hatch in the middle of winter. The carcasses of the adults float downstream to line the banks of the Fraser, symbols of both birth and death.

Most of the Yukon Territory and British Columbia consist of two major mountain chains, the Rockies and the Coastal Range, divided by a broad plateau. This mountain-plateau-mountain system, called the Cordillera, is a colossal labyrinth of deep trenches, steep slopes, broad plains, dark canyons, and a few lush valleys. In the south, the western mountain slopes are richly forested, but the eastern slopes are sheltered from rain and sometimes so dry that only cactus grows. It is not difficult to see why the Cordillera defied settlement or exploration for many years, and why today it is still sparsely settled.

Not all animals, however, quail at the spectacular heights. The bighorn sheep live above the treeline, nimbly reaching the highest and most inaccessible parts of the mountains. With winter's approach in the Rockies, the sheep gather on knolls and rims. Bands of rams pursue solitary ewes over the steep, rocky slopes. It is November, and soon heavy snows will cover the peaks. For sheep, it is mating season.

Their surplus energy finds an outlet in jousting, for ewes as well as rams. The two sheep retreat some distance from each other and charge at full speed. Just before impact, they almost fly through the air, with only their hind feet touching ground. As they collide, they lower their heads and take the full brunt of the impact on their foreheads. The collision of these 800-pound animals is so great that both bighorns wander around dazed for some time. When they recover, they trot back to their starting points and charge again.

Between the mountains of western Canada and the Shield in the east is a large flat basin of land. The southern part of this basin is the Plains, land as monotonous as the Cordillera is dramatic. And it is as large as it is dramatic. Each of the three Plains (or "Prairie") provinces—Alberta, Saskatchewan, and Manitoba—is nearly as large as the state of Texas. The semi-arid grasslands stretch flat and unending, as far as the eye can see.

Yet even the Plains has important variations in vegetation and terrain, from the rolling foothills of the Rockies, which gradually flatten into mixed-grass plains, to the Manitoba Plain, where once was found the great true prairie of Canada.

Few people living today have ever seen true prairie. On true prairie the grass grows very tall, to shoulder height. Today, most of the prairie has been plowed under and turned to agriculture. The remaining grasslands are not prairie but mixed-grass plains with short (six to eight inches) and mid (two to four feet) grasses. Part of the Canadian Plains is so arid that only short grass, sage, and cactus grow.

Winds sweep across the semi-arid Plains unobstructed, raising sandstorms in the short hot summers, whipping snow into blizzards in winter. Hoboes who rode trains back and forth across the treeless miles named it Big Lonely. The sight of the land stretching into the distance and the sky curving down on perfectly even horizons does make one feel alone and small on the earth. Perhaps it is only in such a place that human beings have some idea of how large the world really is.

It is well that we stood in the open for a while, under a big sky, on a big land, for now we leap over the southern part of the Shield that separates the Plains from Central Canada. We leave the "land of land" and find ourselves in the land of people. What strikes us after the Plains is how small this land is, just a little fringe at the base of the Shield, less than 2 percent of the territory of Canada. But this is where most of the people in Canada live.

Central Canada, which comprises the provinces of Ontario and Quebec, was one of the earliest settled areas. The St.

Lawrence River cuts from the Atlantic Ocean deep into Central Canada, which can also be easily reached from the United States, by the Great Lakes. Water determined the settlement pattern of Canada in its early days, and still has a considerable impact on population distribution.

Central Canada was not only accessible to early settlers; it was hospitable as well. The natural tree cover, unlike the dense Boreal Forest, was relatively easy to clear, with little underbrush. The trees had remarkable variety. In addition to Boreal species such as spruce, there was the highly valuable white pine, and in the southern parts, vast stands of deciduous trees: beech, elm, maple, oak. A transition zone between evergreen and deciduous forest, Central Canada has the advantages of both. Because this area lies farther south than any of the rest of Canada, livestock such as dairy cattle and hogs can be raised, and large orchards of apples, cherries, and peaches are grown.

Not that winters are not cold. Even in southern Ontario and Quebec, they are harsh and long, with deep snows and stiff winds. In the large cities concentrated in this area, snow removal is a major problem, requiring a large work force, advanced technology, and constant diligence. The St. Lawrence, so economically important to the region, is closed by ice for four months each year.

Central Canada is divided into two parts—the land along the St. Lawrence, mostly in the province of Quebec, and the land around the Great Lakes, which lies in Ontario. The peoples of these two sections have been at odds with one another for centuries. Today, we might say that it is because one group speaks French and the other English. Long before whites came to America, however, when Iroquoian tribes inhabited these areas, the Iroquoians of the St. Lawrence were constantly at war with those of the Lake country.

Perhaps it has something to do with the land. The St. Lawrence area of Quebec is hemmed in, in the north by the Canadian Shield which forms the Laurentian Mountains, and in the south by the bare Gaspé region. In Ontario, on the other hand, the Shield rises only a few hundred feet. And Ontario's southern boundary is the Great Lakes and the St. Lawrence River, which are main routes of travel. Thus the land of Ontario is conducive to trade, commerce, and communication, both with the interior of Canada and with the United States. The land around the St. Lawrence tends to restrict people to Quebec. Perhaps this difference is as much responsible for antagonism between the peoples as any other factor.

East of Central Canada, in the Maritime provinces of New Brunswick, Nova Scotia, and Prince Edward Island, it is no longer the land which divides people, but the sea. The sea fragments this region into a series of islands and peninsulas, each with its own character. In New Brunswick, the vast forest of white pine has long since been lumbered out, leaving scrubby, stunted woodland, marshes, and struggling farms. The pine and fir of Nova Scotia are straighter, taller. They spread over rounded hills right to the peaceful blue of the Bras d'Or Lakes, and to the shores of the slate-gray Atlantic. On tiny Prince Edward Island, the tidy farms and gentle beaches make this the most pastoral spot in Canada. Along the northern coast lies Labrador, a land of Arctic ice and tundra.

The easternmost land in North America is the island of Newfoundland. The interior of this great island is Boreal Forest; the shores are rocky. Perched on the bare coastline are tiny fishing and mining villages, most of them accessible only by a single poor road or by sea.

The term "Atlantic Provinces" has been coined to include all these areas, but common usage distinguishes between "the Maritimes" and "Newfoundland."

The lobster, a symbol of Nova Scotia, is a tough, battling

creature, a loner, hunting its prey by wit and shrewdness. When first born, it looks more like a louse than a lobster. It floats to the surface of the ocean where it is at the mercy both of surface-feeding fish and its own brothers and sisters, who will seize and eat it if they have a chance. Only one out of 5,000 baby lobsters survive; to win the battle for life a lobster must be intent on eating to avoid being eaten.

The cod of Newfoundland, unlike the lone lobster of the Maritimes, group in shoals each morning in order to feed. While they live mainly on small fish during the summer, in winter they are bottom feeders, eating shrimp, crab, molluscs, and worms. They have very strong digestive juices for the shellfish, and are as voracious as they are indiscriminate; large cod have been found with such articles in their stomachs as keys, candles, a rabbit, and a bound book. At sunset they return to shallow water and disperse for the night, waiting for the sun that will signal them once again to group in shoals.

When winter comes the cod move in to shallow waters, and the lobsters move out to the deeps. Inland, in the Maritimes and Newfoundland, winter brings snow drifts in huge mounds which cover even the rooftops. The winds blow the snow across everything, at times hiding houses, fields, fences, and shrubs, muffling the sounds of people, till all is hushed and white.

Divided into ten provinces and two territories, Canada is as large as the United States and Mexico combined. And most of this area contains fewer people than the great deserts of Africa. The Plains, the Cordillera, the Boreal Forest, the Arctic—each is a vast area, vast and sparsely populated.

Before the advent of Europeans, virtually all of Canada's land was claimed by the Native Peoples Europeans called Indians. Many tribes lived in the Boreal Forest, for instance, and in the Cordillera, and some had even made a highly successful life for themselves in the forbidding Arctic. Thus, while there were fewer people in Canada at that time than now, they were more evenly distributed.

European civilization took root only· in the most temperate parts of Canada, and in dominating the country, disrupted the original pattern. The terrain and climate were obstacles to settlement, barriers to communication. Canada is a vast country, a country of many varied parts—which seem to function separately a good deal of the time. And this separateness is fostered by the physical environment.

The physical difficulties are related mainly to the distance and the cold. The great interior is criss-crossed by an intricate system of rivers and streams. And Canada is blessed with oceans on three sides, from which there are many remarkable natural inlets to the interior: Hudson Bay carves into the Shield; the St. Lawrence reaches across the south; the Yukon and Mackenzie rivers strike through half the northern country. These waterways are ideally situated for encouraging large settlements in the interior. But in winter, all are frozen or blocked by ice.

Another physical feature which results in separateness is that a good deal of Canada is not suited to agricultural development and consequent settlement. It is unlikely that farmers will compete with the bighorns for the Rockies, and uses of the Arctic and Shield still wait to be discovered. Except for a few scattered outposts, practically all Canadians live within 300 miles of the United States border. And the areas which have no agriculture tend to isolate those areas that do from one another.

Yet these are characteristics rather than problems: these are Canada. Canadians have both overcome and adapted to the physical environment. They have adapted by making resources of the "disadvantages." The Boreal Forest, where agriculture is impossible, is the basis for an extensive pulpwood industry; the lightly covered rocks of the Shield invite mining. And after the Industrial

Revolution, the difficulty of distance did not remain insurmountable. Railways, highways, airways—all have helped the separate parts function as one country. The cold itself has advantages, for the long-wintered, short-summered land produces superior strains of grain and livestock.

The resources of a land are "problems" only if there is a lack of them. And climate and space are "problems" only when they are unmanageable. Early European settlers, for instance, faced a hostile environment because they had only the tools and knowledge of the Old World to deal with the strange conditions. By now Canadians know their world and have adjusted to it. No, the problem of Canada is not its resources, but their technological exploitation and economic distribution. And the clash of separate interests is due less to the natural environment than to the human-made one.

Spring comes late to Canada.

It is nearly May before the first ocean vessel can make its way up the St. Lawrence.

When the ice starts breaking in the Boreal Forest streams and lakes, the beaver gives birth to her kits.

And as the snows recede in the Rockies, the bighorn sheep head for those high, hidden mountain meadows, inaccessible to human beings, where the alpine grass and flowers grow in profusion. It is in May that the bighorn ewe retreats to drop her lamb. She climbs to the most remote spot she can find, preferably with a warm southern exposure and a spectacular view of the surrounding country.

It is well into June before the ice breaks up in the Arctic Archipelago; the floes crash and shift with a grating, grinding roar. If it does not have cubs to look after, the polar bear, which is shy of the unstable, thawing ice, sometimes boards an ice floe. It sails south on its private piece of ice, leaving the chaos and noise behind. Eventually the floe melts, sometimes a couple of hundred miles from home, and the polar bear swims back to a calmer environment.

By then the caribou have made their spring migration. En route, some time in June, the cows give birth. They all drop their young within two weeks of each other, and the calves can run a half hour after birth—so the delay in migration is minimal. They cannot stop long; they are heading for the lush spring pasture of open tundra.

The tundra is covered with moss, lichen, and short grass of delicate green. The creepers spurt to life in a flurry of growing, warmed by the sun that shines for weeks on end, never setting. Over 700 kinds of flowers burst into bloom. They grow close to the ground, scattered like stars through the turf, blossoming in white and bright alpine hues of red, blue, yellow. The broad Arctic meadows are thick carpets of light green grass and bright small flowers.

And the sun shines all the time.

THE FIRST PEOPLES

TWO

At one time no people lived on the American continents. Everywhere were animals and plants, some
of them strange to us now, for it was very long
ago. When people first came, they had only the
barest means of existence, the most primitive of
shelter and clothing, the simplest of weapons. In
the new lands they adapted to a great diversity of
animal and plant life and to climates as different as
those of the Arctic and the Amazon. They adapted,
and in the course of thousands of years they developed civilizations which in some areas, such as
Mexico, equaled ancient Egypt in sophistication,
and which in some fields, such as interpreting
dreams and measuring time, surpassed the succeed-

ing European culture in knowledge. The people originated on another continent, but their cultures originated in the Americas.

The first people to discover America were Asians, who crossed a land bridge between Siberia and Alaska during the last Ice Age. They were hunters rather than farmers. Nomads from the beginning, they had no strong attachment to a previous culture and brought little with them. They brought only their bows, their moccasins, and some folk tales. These "Indians" spread out over two American continents, and a few thousand years ago, civilization began to develop.

Civilization in Europe centered around wheat; in the Americas, the agricultural staple was maize, or what present-day Americans call corn, which the Indians developed from a wild grass. Empires grew where maize grew. In North America the great center of civilization was in Mexico. The ideas and culture of Mexico spread north into what is now the United States and eventually, with the Iroquois, into Canada.

But generally, the influence of the great civilizations of the south faded farther north. In the harsh northern climates, there were no great cities. In the north, there was little time for ceremony or socializing, much less building empires—or even waging wars. In only two small parts of Canada was food so abundant that life during the long winter was secure. And virtually all of the country, unlike today, was inhabited.

A quarter of a million people spread over the four million square miles of Canada. This vast territory was claimed by over fifty tribes, each speaking a different language or dialect, each having its own culture developed over thousands of years. Most of them, because of the scanty livelihood in these lands, met in bands or joined as a tribe only at certain times of the year, if at all. They had no large political structure, no cities, and no leisure class. The cultures that evolved were based on an individual, migratory way of life. But after thousands of years most of these cultures were highly developed.

And this cultural development did not depend upon a temperate climate or ease of living. In the farthest reaches of the north, on the barren ice pack of the Arctic, the Innuit (meaning simply "The People," singular Innuk), or Eskimos as they are often called, developed one of the most successful cultures in the world.

The Innuit relied principally on the seal, which they speared from the edge of the ice or from their one-person kayaks. Or they stalked it over the ice, mimicking the movements of the seal until close enough to strike. During the winter, they waited long cold hours at the seal's breathing hole, watching for it to surface. When the ice broke up in the summer, the Innuit again took to the sea, fishing for salmon as well as the seal and attacking even the mighty whale. Their whaling techniques were at least as sophisticated as those of Europeans of that time.

The Innuit also hunted caribou in the summer, for caribou were as indispensable to their way of life as the sea animals were. Sewing, which parts of the caribou made possible, was an occupation equaled in importance only by hunting and fishing. The Innuit woman created an outfit which not only kept a hunter warm in temperatures below $-50°F.$, which not only was waterproof in the freezing Arctic waters, but which also weighed something less than five pounds. The supreme importance of the stitchery required for this efficient clothing gave women an equal place with men in the Innuit culture.

The Innuit were artisans of the first order. Their major dwelling—the snow-house, or "igloo"—is an elegant example. It was virtually draft-proof, heavily insulated, and could be built in a few hours, using a material readily available almost everywhere in the northern Arctic. The hunting and fishing implements they invented would take several pages just to list. They carved toys and amulets, needle cases, thimble holders, handles and points for weapons and tools, all manner of small gadgets and devices, all made with great care and craft. Ivory and stone carving, in fact, developed into a true art, and through modern times, their unique

style, which often represents animals in round, fluid lines, is easily identified.

The Innuit—and most Native Peoples in Canada, for that
matter—owed their leisure to the very harshness of their environment. It was during the long winter, when the day lasts only a few
hours, that the Innuk was forced home from hunting by the im-
penetrable dark. Then would be the time to flash across the snow
in dogsleds to neighboring igloos to dance and sing and spin tales.
Then would be the time to carve by the oil lamp, to study a stone
for hours, seeking the animal that lay hidden in its shape. Then
would be the time to imagine and to ponder, to remember the
awful darkness of the sea and of the night.

Their demons were the dark and the sea. To be lost in the
long night, in a vast world of bare ice, was a fearful thing, and
their religion held a whole host of malevolent spirits that reached
from the night to take possession. Their principal deity, however,
was the sea-goddess Sedna, who controlled the ice and the seals,
and hence their lives.

The only laws were age-old taboos and a general sense of
justness, but this anarchy worked because the Innuit had common
aims and need of one another. Crime was usually the result of
temper or vengeance, rather than greed, for they were a sharing
people. A successful hunter always divided the catch with a less
fortunate companion, knowing that the world was a vast, lonely
place and that the time would come when one's own luck would
turn.

The principal livelihood of most Canadian Native Peoples,
with the exception of the Iroquois, was hunting and fishing. The
Indians who inhabited the great Boreal Forest relied mainly on
trapping and snaring. Theirs was perhaps the poorest economy,
for forest—unlike the sea—is not bountiful. The small furred
animals that scurry through the trees are barely enough for one
meal and part of one moccasin lining. The large animals that live
in the Forest at least part of the year, such as caribou and moose,

scatter to forage in ones or twos, protected by the heavy brush. Trapping was surer than the bow and arrow, and the Forest peoples excelled in this, snaring everything from mink to moose.

Nevertheless, in winter starvation was not uncommon, especially in the harsh northwestern Forest. And the first to starve were the women. Women had no economic independence in this part of Canada, and in some tribes they were virtually slaves. Separated from males at an early age, tabooed during adolescence, married shortly thereafter, the women dragged toboggans through snow in the winter and in summer packed the heavy hides on backs. Mothers sometimes killed their female infants to spare them such a life.

The Boreal Forest covers a huge area, and there were many differences between the woodland tribes. Yet their similarities are more striking than their differences. Most wore typical Forest clothes—shirt or kilt, leggings and moccasins, to which would be added mittens, hat, and robe for winter—all of which required eight to ten caribou or deer skins. Forest dwellings were made of the most plentiful resource, trees, and the most popular shape everywhere was the conical lodge, called a "wigwam." Likewise, transportation was fairly standard: snowshoes for walking in winter and toboggans for dragging hides and household goods on their frequent moves. And in summer, when the numerous streams and lakes of the Forest were free from ice, they used canoes.

Amazingly light, the bark canoe could be portaged long distances by a single adult. It was quite sturdy, and if perchance it were ripped by a rock or floating timber, it could be repaired with a strip of bark, a few threads of spruce root to sew on the bark, and a little spruce gum to cover the seams. It was perhaps the most elegant contribution of a people who had a harder life and more desperate circumstances than even the Innuit of the Arctic.

The difference between the peoples of the Boreal Forest and the peoples of the Pacific Coast seems the difference between night and day. On the narrow strip of coast developed a culture that built huge "longhouses" which were perhaps 200 by 50 feet, standing 20 feet high, and housing as many as 50 occupants. Here on the Coast was the leisure for art, and the Pacific Coast Indians made delicately carved plates of slate, silver bracelets, huge "totem" poles with highly stylized animal figures, and wood boxes so well built they held water. And here on the bountiful Coast were the leisure and wealth for a ritual so wasteful it would have shocked the Forest peoples.

Called a "potlatch," it was a huge party in the course of which the host would give as many goods as possible to the guests; sometimes in a burst of competitiveness, the host might even destroy valuable possessions. We have indeed gone from an economy of scarcity to an economy of abundance.

In the temperate climate of the Pacific Coast, trees such as cedar and fir grew to great heights. In the Pacific Ocean numerous animals such as sea otter and whale were available in large quantities. And up the rivers that fed into the ocean ran five species of salmon and the eulachon, or "candlefish," which was so highly prized for its oil. To interrupt the runs of salmon, the Indians used weirs (woven fences), which were built, worked, and shared by the whole community. Theirs was certainly a land of plenty, and they developed a social structure of clans and rituals far beyond what the scattered living of the Boreal Forest peoples could support.

This social structure was imported inland, into the rough mountains, plateaus, and gorges of the Cordillera. The Cordillera Indians traded extensively between the Pacific Coast peoples to the west and the Forest and Plains Indians to the east, and so combined several cultures. The headwaters of the great rivers that feed into the Pacific were in their territory, and like the Pacific Coast peoples, they celebrated the first shoals of salmon with potlatches. On the other hand, many of the tribes left their mountains during buffalo season to hunt with the Plains Indians, and like the peoples of the Plains they gave their chief more importance than did most Canadian Indians.

Not all of the characteristics of the Cordillerans were borrowed. More than other Canadian Indians they wove baskets, some of them so tightly they held water. And they had a unique dwelling, which was half dug into the ground and reached by a ladder through the roof. Their rugged terrain, which required them to trade extensively and thus be affected by other Indian cultures, also caused them to be one of the last peoples "discovered" by white civilization and changed by it.

East of the Cordillera were the Plains, and the peoples who inhabited this area were affected by white civilization very early— at first in a positive sense. The horse and gun were brought by the Spaniards to the Americas, and they quickly spread northward to the Canadian Plains. With the horse and gun, the Indians could kill buffalo efficiently and dramatically. Their wealth increased and their culture blossomed.

Most of the Plains, one of the greatest grasslands the world has ever known, provided lush graze for buffalo and antelope. The buffalo ranged in large herds, in the thousands. In winter they migrated out to the territory, and disappeared. Then in spring, as if by magic, they returned.

Before they acquired horses and guns, the Plains Indians shot buffalo on foot, with stone-pointed arrows which broke if they struck bone. This was dangerous work. As long as the people straggled in small families and hunted alone, they had little success. Gradually they learned to form larger groups, tribes. Then they could herd the buffalo into wooden pounds or over cliffs, as a community.

This had to be done with a great deal of group coordination, and so the Plains Indians—from their very beginnings—had a strong sense of "community" or tribe. In winter, they again scattered, living off small game such as rabbit, and pemmican—a pounded mixture of dried buffalo meat, fat, and berries.

The Plains people borrowed from the east the most practical housing for their windy Plains, the conical wigwam, which they covered with buffalo hides. As many as two dozen hides might be required for one lodge, and before the horse made buffalo cheap, this dwelling was the most prized possession. The women built and sewed the lodges, and were generally considered the owners. They improved the wigwam so that it is distinguished from similar structures in Canada by the name "tepee."

On the Plains, the hunting dog was developed into a traction animal before the advent of the horse. When the people moved, the poles of the tepee were tied to either side of the dog; the ends that trailed behind were joined by rawhide straps. On this *travois* were piled the household possessions and the hides. Several dogs were required for each family.

With the coming of the horse, more Indians moved out onto the Plains—Indians with different cultures, different tongues. The original Plains culture easily absorbed these new arrivals because of the strong community organization which already existed. But all in all, it was a fairly simple, often scratchy existence, with only the beginnings of an exciting culture. Until the horse.

In the Atlantic Ocean area, the predominantly woodland way of life was modified by the sea. There were three important peoples: the Malecite, the Micmac, and the Beothuk.

The Malecite inhabited the strip along the St. Lawrence estuary, from the Iroquoian-held lowlands to the beginning of the Gaspé Peninsula. They were neighbors to both the New England Indians and the Iroquois, and it is not surprising that they practiced agriculture, though it was more in the manner of the New Englanders than the Iroquoians. Like the New England Algonkians, they depended as much on woodland hunting as on maize.

The Micmac ("Allies") inhabited the true Maritime area, the Gaspé Peninsula, New Brunswick, Nova Scotia including Cape Breton Island, and Prince Edward Island. Like latter-day Maritimers, their isolation seemed to foster defiant independence.

Their dialect, though Algonkian, was different from neighboring Algonkians, and suggests that they may originally have been part of the Plains Blackfoot nation. They were unfriendly with every tribe nearby.

In winter, they hunted deer, moose, caribou, and smaller game such as porcupine and beaver; in summer they fished at the mouths of rivers and sealed along the Coast. And they dug clams from which they made wampum, the beads used by many eastern tribes for money and record-keeping. Designs on clothing and cradle boards made use of this wampum, as well as of porcupine-quill embroidery and painting.

The Beothuk Indians who inhabited Newfoundland Island were undoubtedly quite similar to the Micmac in their livelihood. Beothuk canoes were unlike those of any other tribes, except the Micmac who copied from these Newfoundlanders. In profile, the canoe resembled a crescent moon, rising to sharp points at both ends. Covered in birch-bark, it was broader, more tub-like than the Forest canoe, and was better suited to rough ocean jaunts than the slender, responsive craft of mainland Canada.

Deep in the interior of Newfoundland, the Beothuk had semi-permanent winter villages, to which the same families returned year after year. These were usually built near large lakes or rivers, where the deer crossed in the fall and could be shot for food.

The Beothuk smeared their bodies and hair with grease, mixed with red ochre, the original purpose being to confound the insects that tormented every living thing during summer. But these Indians also seemed to have a genuine fondness for the color red; they smeared their canoes, lodges, and implements with the ochre. For this reason they were called "Red Indians" by early settlers. It is clear that Beothuk women had status, independence, and respect. More than that, we do not know. Shortly after the coming of the Europeans, the Beothuk were nearly extinct.

Almost all of the Canadian Indians had one thing in common: their sensitivity to animals. This was true among the Innuit, who carved their stone and ivory into polar bears and birds; it was true among the Boreal Forest tribes, who chose for their spirits and good luck charms the beasts of the Forest; it was true on the Pacific Coast, where the Indians for all their abundance and leisure and sophistication, chose animals for the motifs in their art and everyday material goods; it was true on the Canadian Plains, where the Indians recognized the buffalo cycle and lived by it.

There is only one Native People in Canada for whom animals were not economically all-important, the Iroquoians. And they were different from other Canadians in several ways. In most Indian bands, the burden of livelihood rested with the males. In the Iroquoian society, it was the women who provided most of the food. The men traded, warred, and did some hunting and fishing. They also cleared fields from the forest and built longhouses for the women.

The women were farmers. They raised squashes, tobacco, fifteen varieties of corn, sixty varieties of beans. They also gathered wild berries, herbs and greens, and maple sap. Their corn was the staple, securing a living from year to year instead of day to day. Thus the women provided the social foundation. And the fields, produce, longhouse, and children belonged to them.

The maize-growing Iroquoians were perhaps the northernmost people to show the influence of the powerful Mexican civilization. Some authorities believe that they had migrated slowly from Mexico through the southeast United States and into Central Canada. Since the surrounding Boreal Forest could not support agriculture and prevented further advance, they were limited to the area along the St. Lawrence and the region around the Great Lakes. They were more aggressive than the neighboring Forest peoples, and the efficiency of their agriculture allowed the men ample time to organize political systems and to war.

Eventually, they even came to fight among themselves. The five nations along the St. Lawrence—Cayuga, Mohawk, Oneida, Onondaga, and Seneca—formed the powerful Iroquois Con-

federacy. Their cousins around the Great Lakes reacted by forming their own confederacy, the Wendat, or Huron. The two peoples were fairly evenly matched, and the small-scale hostilities
might have continued indefinitely, with neither side doing the
other much harm. But then the Europeans brought the gun.

If there is one generalization we can make about Canadian
Indians, it is that they maintained more contact with the land than
Mexican Indians did. And their art when it developed—among the
Innuit and on the Pacific Coast, for instance—was related to animals of the land and sea, rather than to geometric patterns, as
among southern peoples. Their religions and rituals, too, revolved
more around animals than around the sun or sky or universe. The
Canadian Indians belonged to their land, and the land to them, in
a way in which the European immigrants—who were already attached to a well-developed civilization when they arrived—did
not, and might never.

Many of the Indian cultures would certainly have evolved
further. But they probably would not have developed politically in
the manner of European countries—that is, into feudalism—for
they differed on one fundamental premise. They felt strongly that
land was common, that it belonged to all their kind. Quite willing
to vie with other tribes for lucrative hunting grounds, among their
own group they shared, and where enough food existed to support
unproductive members of their bands, they provided for the lame
and elderly.

No individual was permitted to hoard or tax at the expense of
others. Their leaders lived as others did. No wars were ever
fought for the glory of a civil chief. If battle were called for, a
respected warrior was usually appointed as a temporary leader.
Civil government, where it existed, and war were separate business.

Because of the astounding specialization of many of the Indians, it is hard to remember that they were a people without
metal, without the wheel or the horse. With such simple techno-

logical introductions as iron, for instance, and with the coming of
the horse, some of the cultures flared to magnificent accomplishment.

But this happened only in regions where European technology preceded the Europeans. It seems as if these technological
revolutions barely took hold before the white conquest, before the
native cultures were crippled. First stimulated, they were then
overwhelmed.

The Native Peoples are by no means lost—their numbers in
fact are increasing, and despite poverty and persecution and massacre, they have stubbornly clung to what culture they could. In
some ways they are like the Arctic plants, the stems of which die
in winter that the root might live. In the brief summer, they
bloom quickly and close to the ground, bursting into bright hues
of color before the long winter.

EUROPE LOOKS WESTWARD

THREE

The first Europeans to reach American shores were perhaps Irish. A colony which appears to have been Irish is referred to in old Scandinavian sagas, in the earliest Icelandic mariner guides, and in the reports of Scandinavian sailors shipwrecked on Canadian shores.

We do know that a group of Irish monks and fishers was driven from islands off the Irish coast by the great Scandinavian invasion of Europe, and that they made a new settlement in Iceland. And we know that sometime between A.D. 850 and 875, the Scandinavians reached Iceland and drove the Irish group farther west. Some historians think the location of the new Irish colony was Cape Breton

Island, among the Micmacs. By the time of Columbus's discovery, however, the little group had been absorbed into the native environment.

Meanwhile, the Scandinavian population of Iceland had increased to 20,000. In 981, a Norwegian of fierce courage and murderous temperament, Eric the Red, was driven out of Iceland for his quarrels. He founded his own settlement on the large island to the west. With an admirable sense of public relations, he named this treeless land "Greenland." The colony he founded probably numbered 1,000 people by around A.D. 1000 when a shipowner named Bjarni Herjulfsson was blown off course and sighted the thick woods of North America.

As the population on Greenland grew, the lack of timber became critical, and sometime between 1000 and 1004, Eric's son Leif was sent to explore along Herjulfsson's route. Exactly where Leif Ericson and his thirty-odd men landed is disputable, but most authorities favor Nova Scotia or Newfoundland as the "Vinland" mentioned in old Norse sagas. The longest-lived colony in Vinland (lasting three years) was started around 1010 by Thorfinn Karlsefni. His wife Gudrid bore the first known European child on American soil, a son named Snorri.

The Vikings left no permanent impression on America, and America at this time made no impression on Europe. It was still beyond the reach of most European ships and navigation. More important, there simply was not enough pressure in Europe to justify exploration. That would wait on changing economic circumstances.

By 1492, the population of Europe was at full capacity, and the land was fully exploited. The average commoner lived no better, no longer, than the American Indian. Europeans had metals, the wheel, draft animals. For the peasant, this meant a plow, a pot, and perhaps an ox-cart. It usually did not mean a horse.

In one respect the average European was not so well off as the Indian: the commoner had no land. Even the impoverished

Boreal Indians had their own hunting territories, the chiefs no more than the others. In Europe the "chiefs" owned not only all the cultivated land, but also all the "wild" land. Nobles maintained huge forests for their pleasure, and a commoner who poached on these lands risked death. The feudal system of land ownership, however, had allowed great power to accumulate among the nobility. Now the feudal system was being superseded by mercantilism, and a new source of wealth and power was to be found in commerce.

With the Crusades, Europe became dramatically aware of the tantalizing wealth of the Far East. Unfortunately, the tortuous journey by land made expeditions nearly impossible. The nobles and merchants began pressing for a sea route. Merchant banded with merchant—usually according to town or port—in order to outfit the expensive explorations by sea. The thrust of this effort was first directed around the African continent. Those countries that lay in the path of this route—Italy, Portugal, and Spain—produced the great sea captains, pilots, and navigators of the time. As for the captains and navigators, they hired out to whoever would finance them. Thus was the Italian Columbus in the hire of the Spanish Queen. And thus did another Italian, John Cabot, owe his allegiance to the merchants of Bristol, England.

Cabot was the first official discoverer of the Canadian coast. He touched Canada in 1497, possibly near Cape Breton, and sailed back to England convinced that Japan was within reach. Other explorers were sent, for Europe's rulers hoped that, even if there were no Northwest Passage to the Orient, there would be gold such as the Spanish had found to the south. These voyages eventually mapped the coastline and established North America as a continent, but no European had yet explored the Canadian interior.

Then the French King, Francis I, engaged a shipowner and pilot from St. Malo, Jacques Cartier, to search for passage to the Pacific. In 1534, Cartier erected a cross on Penouille Point in the

Bay of Gaspé, claiming the land for France. But the actual exploration of "Canada"—so-called by Cartier from the Mohawk word for "village"—had to wait until the following year. Cartier returned in 1535 and entered the St. Lawrence. Past where the great Saguenay River empties into the St. Lawrence, he came to the Mohawk village of Stadacona (later Quebec).

Then he pressed on up the St. Lawrence to the Huron town of Hochelaga (later Montreal). It was an impressive town, with fifty longhouses and a triple palisade. The whole setting was dominated by a mountain, which Cartier named *Mont Réal* (Royal Mount). From its heights he saw the Lachine Rapids, which prevented further passage up the St. Lawrence. He returned to Stadacona and spent a terrible winter there before sailing for France.

We wonder today why for a good century after Cartier, the merchants of France, England, and Holland continued to waste expeditions on the forbidding coasts. The cost in money and lives was extravagant. With the most favorable of winds, the journey across the Atlantic took twenty days; with storms it might take a couple of months. That left precious little time to explore, hit-and-miss, a completely unknown coastline before winter set in.

And the Europeans were quite unprepared for a Canadian winter. Cartier lost a quarter of his men to winter scurvy. An expedition led by Jens Munck, stranded for the winter of 1619–20 in Hudson Bay, had three survivors out of sixty-five.

In the long run, however, these voyages precipitated a revolution. They brought shipbuilding, sailing, and navigation to new stages of development. They mapped the outlines of eastern and northern Canada. And they spread news of a marvelous fishing ground off Newfoundland. The expeditions came and went, found no gold, no Northwest Passage. But the fishing boats that flocked in their wake became a permanent feature.

Basque and Portuguese fishers in fact had been going to the Grand Banks off Newfoundland before many of the explorers, probably before Cabot and even Columbus. The Basque fishers of St.-Jean-de-Luz, in defending their rights in 1624, claimed their fleet had established a fishery there "more than three centuries ago." That would bring their "discovery" to about the time of the invention of the mariner's compass, and is therefore plausible.

Quite possibly, America was not discovered by Irish mystics, nor Viking adventures, nor Italian navigators, but by modest fishers. And although it received less fanfare than the search for gold and spices, the fishing industry was more important to Europe's economy than gold, for fish was vital as a staple protein.

Any particular season would find hundreds of boats off the Newfoundland coast. It was an international occupation, and ports all along the west coast of Europe sent fleets. There were Basques from St.-Jean-de-Luz; there were Portuguese, Spanish, and Dutch. They came from Bristol, London, Barnstaple, and Poole in England. In France, their home ports included St. Malo, La Rochelle, Dieppe, and Rouen.

Each captain was master of a boat, and each fleet was loyal only to its own home port. The captain of the first boat to reach Newfoundland at the beginning of the season was declared "Admiral"; he was in charge of apportioning the fishing grounds. He actually had little to do; the fishing grounds were pretty much determined by tradition. And certainly there was enough for everyone.

While fish dominated Newfoundland, fur was settling New France. The first fur trade began as an amateur occupation— fishers picking up a little extra "cash" before returning home. Then about the middle of the sixteenth century, felt-makers discovered that beaver fur made the best hats, for it had an exceptionally lustrous finish. Large felt hats from beaver became the rage of Europe. Then *la traite*—the beaver fur trade—became a deadly serious affair.

Pioneered by individual traders and fishers, *la traite* soon at-

tracted the big money in Europe. At first, the company vessels
from Europe skirted the coasts. By the end of the sixteenth century, they had entered the St. Lawrence and discovered Tadoussac, an ancient trade center of the Indians. By the early seventeenth century, the Europeans were thinking in terms of
permanent posts. Beaver fur determined the distribution of settlement, and to this day it is the beaver, doomed by the fashion of a
faraway land, that symbolizes the conquest of Canada. Within
seventy years, Canada was transformed from a trading post into a
colony.

Both France and England, in accordance with the economic
theories of the day, originally left settlement in the hands of the
merchants and companies. The King or Queen retained ultimate
feudal rights (without investing any money), and the Company got
use-ownership of the land, authorization to arrest or tax anyone
trading in the territory of its monopoly, most of the profit, and the
responsibility of colonizing. With these advantages, it would seem
these enterprises could not possibly fail. But fail most of them
did.

The monarchs, who wanted more lands, and the Church,
which wanted more converts, were interested in genuine settlement. The companies to whom they left such settlement, however, were interested in profits, not settlement.

In the first attempt at colonization, that of the Seigneur de
Roberval in 1541, for instance, the main concern was for the leg-
endary gold of the north. De Roberval's "settlers," including five
women, were culled from prisons and alleyways and forced into
service. He maintained discipline by meting out appalling punishments. Not finding riches, he and his "colony" returned to France
after only a year.

Legend has it, however, that he left behind his young niece
Marguerite, and her fate is a measure of the man's character. As
they approached the coast on their way to Canada, de Roberval

discovered Marguerite was in love with a young man on board.
He had her and her maid put off on a small deserted island. Her
lover jumped ship and swam after her. They built a rude shelter
on the island, where Marguerite gave birth to a baby. Her maid,
her lover, and her baby all succumbed to the rigorous climate.
Marguerite survived for two years, fending off wild animals,
fierce winters, and hallucinations, before a fishing boat found
her.

The de Roberval expedition seemed to curse the various colonization attempts for the next half century. Then in 1604, Pierre
du Guast, Sieur de Monts, was granted the area which is now
roughly the Maritime provinces, but which then was called Acadia. His party included the man who was to become the founder
of New France, and hence Canada, Samuel Champlain.

Between 1604 and 1607, de Monts and Champlain, with the
help of the Micmac Indians, established a permanent colony on
the Bay of Fundy, which they named Port Royal. But the two men
realized that, while Acadia was ideal for agriculture, the greatest
concentration of furs lay inland, along the St. Lawrence. The
ideal spot was a commanding bluff above the St. Lawrence named
Québec from the Algonkian word for "where the river narrows."
On July 3, 1608, Champlain established his fur-trading post. And
there Quebec sat, perched on its bluff, awaiting furs from the Indians, supplies from de Monts, and soldiers from the King.

Champlain had barely established himself in New France
before he was involved in native politics. The St. Lawrence furs
came from the north and west, and were transported east and
south toward the Atlantic. The Indians along the route, particularly the Huron of the Great Lakes, became entrepreneurs between
the trapping peoples inland and the Europeans near the coast. As
they commanded the north shore of the St. Lawrence, Champlain
forged a solid alliance with them. He began a practice which was
to become the mainstay of the French fur trade: he sent a youth,

Étienne Brûlé, to live among them. Brûlé was the first of countless young men who turned Indian out of choice and who,
through periodic contact with white settlements, paved the way
for the French fur traders, called *coureurs de bois*.

But the five nations of the Iroquois Confederacy commanded
the south shore of the St. Lawrence and were deadly enemies of
their cousins, the Huron. Champlain was forced to choose sides
between Iroquois and Huron. Considering the location of Quebec,
he had no choice. Rather than allow his allies, the Huron, to be
intercepted in bringing him furs, he took up arms against the
Iroquois.

Indian hostilities were only one of Champlain's problems.
The other was the lack of support from France. The sponsorship
of his trading post transferred from de Monts (who was defeated
back in France by competitors) to the Comte de Soissons (who
died) to Prince Henri de Condé (who fell out with the Queen
Regent). The companies that followed failed to nurture the colony. Promises of support dribbled to nothing. *La traite* was quite
prosperous, turning 15,000–20,000 pelts a year, but none of the
profits went back into settlement.

At the end of 1628, after twenty years of effort, Quebec was
still a trading post. Only five families of laborers were settled on
the post, and only two persons—one a woman—had farms. The
population of less than a hundred (including the twenty or thirty
youths who lived among the Indians) was mainly involved in tran-
sient occupations. They included laborers for Champlain's forts,
clerks and agents for the Company, interpreters, soldiers, and
missionaries of the Récollet religious order.

Then in 1628, the first ox-drawn plow broke land in the new
colony, heralding the changes in fortune which mark this year.
One of the most important changes was that the Récollets, who
were dependent on the measly handouts of the Company, invited
the powerful Jesuit Order to join their mission. The Jesuits at that

time enjoyed enormous influence in high places. Unusually well-educated and energetic, they had the wealthiest order in Christendom, and received handsome contributions for their work from the nobility. They brought Quebec large financial gifts which, in some lean years, virtually sustained the colony. And such "gifts" literally built the city of Quebec.

The Jesuits also contributed some of the most dramatic martyrdoms in history, for they were fearless in establishing missions. Father Brébeuf, for instance, was one of the first Jesuits to arrive in 1625. His main occupation for the next twenty years was establishing missions among the Huron. In the Iroquois offensive against the Huron in 1649, Brébeuf refused to flee and was captured. A hearty man, he withstood appalling tortures for a day before dying. Another, Father Jogues, ventured among the hostile Mohawks to establish a mission. Taken prisoner by the Iroquois and badly mutilated, he managed to escape—and then stubbornly returned to try again, only to be killed by the Mohawks. The Jesuits established for all time the Catholic Church in Canada. And their role in the 1600s was absolutely vital in modifying the narrow interests of the companies.

Political power in France, meanwhile, was becoming centralized. Under Louis XIII, France decided to take responsibility for colonizing out of the hands of the mercantile companies.

In 1627, Louis's brilliant advisor, Cardinal de Richelieu, founded the Company of New France, also called The Hundred Associates for the number of its subscribers. The Company outfitted the most generous colonization effort to date: four ships bearing 400 settlers. Unfortunately, Richelieu neglected to provide a naval escort, and the whole enterprise was lost.

France at this time was fighting with England. An English flotilla entered the St. Lawrence and captured as its first prize three of the four bounteous ships belonging to The Hundred Associates. It then took the small post at Miscou and the large post at

Tadoussac. On July 9, 1628, Admiral David Kirke anchored before Quebec.

Champlain refused the courteous terms offered by Kirke and held out for nearly a year. After a dreadful winter and lean spring, the inhabitants began to despair. When Kirke and his brothers returned and again offered terms the next July, Champlain accepted. The English allowed the few French settlers who worked the land to stay, and took the rest aboard to be repatriated in France.

Six days later the first French ship bringing help slipped past the blockade, only to lock horns with Kirke's ship farther upstream—literally lock horns, for the two ships entangled their masts during the furious battle, and were so stuck until the French surrendered—all this with Champlain and his companions imprisoned in the hold below. The irony is that just three years later, France and England signed a treaty, returning Quebec to France.

Champlain again took possession of Quebec in 1633, and colonization finally began. The Hundred Associates, unable since their catastrophic loss to finance colonization, introduced the seigneurial system, whereby *habitants* (or "farmers") were organized by *seigneurs* (or "landlords"). Although the land was "owned" in the feudal sense by the *seigneur,* in effect each *habitant* had a farm, or *habitation.* These farms fronted the river for water and ran back from the St. Lawrence like ribbons. Thus they became known as "strip" farms.

Once the *habitation* was established, it might produce melons, squash, pumpkin, peas, corn, beans, and grain. Much of the farming, of course, was learned from the Huron. The Indians also taught settlers how to gather maple sap, where to find greens, how to use medicinal herbs. The staples were beef, which was raised domestically from cattle shipped from Europe, and the game, fish, and birds which the settlers hunted. The unbounded wilderness was one of the most important assets for the new settlers: back in Europe there was no place to roam; here in New France, there was a whole continent. Quebec grew steadily.

Champlain lived to see the first genuine thrust of settlement, which began in 1634. He lived to see the first real settlers disembark, find their strips, and break ground. He died in 1635, having completed his life's work, the establishment of New France.

THIRTY CRUCIAL YEARS

FOUR

During the first half of the seventeenth century,
France and England were engaged in continuous ri-
valry. Their maneuvers in Europe affected France's
holdings in the New World a great deal.

By 1633, the French were established in three
areas of North America: New France, to which
Champlain had returned two years before his death;
Newfoundland, still an international territory
frequented only during fishing season; and Acadia,
which had been growing as an agricultural and fur
colony for nearly thirty years. It was in France's
first American colony, Acadia, that her colonial
policy first showed its weakness.

Acadia had a solid fur trade and thriving fisheries. It also had a great deal of cultivable land, and a number of small farmers had been quietly going about their business since the first settlement in 1604. Furthermore, Acadia had an enviable geographical position, leading the North American continent into the Atlantic, and lying between New France and New England. These advantages made it both desirable and vulnerable: the Dutch and the English pressed from the south.

The Puritans landed at Plymouth sixteen years after the French settled Acadia. Unlike France, England lost no time in encouraging its new colony. Within two decades, the population of New England was 40,000. France, on the other hand, tended to discourage initiative on the part of its colonies. The results were disastrous.

After de Monts and Champlain left Acadia to found New France, the entire fur trade passed into the hands of two youths who had not yet reached the age of twenty: Jean de Biencourt, the son of one of de Monts's friends, and Charles de La Tour, the son of one of Champlain's soldier-laborers. The two young men handled their little business very efficiently, and the fur trade in Acadia flourished. Around 1623, Biencourt died and Charles de La Tour, then about thirty, took over the whole operation.

La Tour lived simply and developed his trade within the Micmac community. He married a Micmac, by whom he had three children. Leaving the settlers to their quiet farming, he ran his fur post with only twenty French. His single problem was the French companies that held fur monopolies. Company vessels continually harassed him. But his three little ships became quite adroit at dodging them.

Then Sir William Alexander of Scotland was granted Nova Scotia by England's James I, despite French settlement. To finance his domain, Alexander sold forty-three baronetcies in Acadia, and dumped seventy Scots settlers, including the baronets, at Port Royal. In late 1629, he allied with David Kirke (who had captured Quebec that summer) to take over the fur trade.

La Tour, for whom dodging the official French ships was but a minor headache, became nervous. The time had come, he decided, to seek official recognition from France. He sent his father Claude across the Atlantic with a petition, pointing out that with France's recognition, he could forcibly evict the Scots. Richelieu and The Hundred Associates sent Claude de La Tour packing.

On his way home, a remarkable accident befell Claude. The ship on which he traveled was captured by none other than David Kirke. It was a lucky accident for Kirke, too, for the Scots had done little with Port Royal. He escorted La Tour to London. La Tour, one of the founders of Acadia, had been treated like a cur in France. But oh, the treatment he received in London! There he was fêted at Court, offered control of Acadia, offered in fact the hand of a Queen's attendant. Sir Alexander even threw in two of his baronetcies, one for Claude and one for Charles. Back in Port Royal with his bride by October 1629, Claude speedily ratified the new agreement with his son.

Then much to their amazement, France came courting. Regretting now their hasty dispatch of the La Tours, The Hundred Associates sent a couple of ships in 1631. Well aware of the agreement with the English, they chose to ignore it, hoping to woo La Tour. They were *very* interested in his enterprise, they assured him. And oh yes, they were sending out supplies to him— foodstuffs, weapons, settlers. They even appointed Charles de La Tour Lieutenant-General of Acadia. They did add one tiny little warning not to be "deceived" by the English. Charles de La Tour replied solemnly that he would choose death rather than stoop to such knavery.

His timing was excellent: in March 1632, the English returned both Quebec and Acadia to the French.

In colonizing Acadia, however, the French government ignored La Tour. The settlers, foodstuffs, etc., arrived with Isaac de Razilly, Richelieu's cousin. Furthermore, Razilly was appointed

Lieutenant-General of Acadia. That made one Lieutenant-General too many.

Razilly and La Tour were instructed to split the land and fur profits. It was an impossible agreement from the beginning. Razilly died the same year as Champlain, 1635, and his colony passed to the Sieur d'Aulnay-Charnisay, who proved even more aggressive than Razilly. The conflict became a feud. The French government, of course, sided with d'Aulnay and ordered him to arrest La Tour.

La Tour meanwhile had established very good relations with The Hundred Associates. In view of his changed circumstances, he took a middle-class French wife, and became one of the few traders to bring the Company solid profits. D'Aulnay, on the other hand, had formed a subsidiary fur company which was trying to push the One Hundred Associates out of the area. So despite the French government, the Company of New France quietly sided with La Tour.

After evading arrest for three years, La Tour was finally blockaded at Saint John. Just when it seemed he would have to surrender, his wife appeared with a ship from France: The Hundred Associates had listened to her pleas and sent help. When night fell, they slipped a rowboat to La Tour.

He went to Boston where he was treated as a guest of honor and even accompanied the Governor to church. He received soldiers, ships, and cannon, with which he led an unsuccessful English attack on Port Royal. The French government howled for his head.

Then while La Tour was back in Boston, d'Aulnay led an assault on Saint John. Mme. La Tour organized a fierce defense, and her small staff killed twelve of d'Aulnay's men before she was captured. She died a prisoner in 1645.

In early 1646, La Tour convinced his old acquaintance David Kirke to lend him his personal flyboat, *The Planter*. Some Boston merchants eagerly outfitted the boat to attack Acadia, and La Tour set sail. In a moment of inspiration, he and his French sailors seized the ship, put the English sailors ashore, and fled to Quebec. There he was received as a hero for avenging Kirke's conquest of 1629. He stayed in Quebec for the next four years.

D'Aulnay's canoe overturned in 1650, and he was found clinging to the upturned bottom of it, frozen to death. That winter, La Tour, fugitive from French justice, was warmly welcomed by the French government. With d'Aulnay dead, he was their best bet in Acadia. All charges were dismissed, and he was reappointed Lieutenant-General. To cap it off, he returned to Acadia and married d'Aulnay's widow in 1653, in order to forestall any claims from the deceased man's heirs. All, it seemed, was settled.

Then the English attacked. They took Saint John, razed Port Royal, and returned to London with La Tour a prisoner. Recalling his Scots baronetcy, and giving a brilliant speech on his own behalf, La Tour worked out a deal that involved London, Boston, and Acadia. He retired to Acadia, where he died in 1663 of old age, apparently with an easy conscience.

History books seldom mention La Tour without calling him a traitor to France. Actually it was France that set itself against La Tour. The Hundred Associates found him honorable in his dealings with them, and supported him when France was calling for his head. To label him a traitor at a time in history when princes were bought and sold is to be hypocritical. He was simply a commoner who, refusing to let himself be ruined by the wars of great nations, looked to his own interests and held his own land.

The hostilities in Europe during the first half of the seventeenth century also affected Newfoundland. Till then, both France and England had been reluctant to settle this land; like the sea from which it got its wealth, Newfoundland was a sort of international territory. But the individualism which worked well in times of peace turned to chaos in wartime. In Acadia hostilities took the form of trespassing; in Newfoundland it was a matter of piracy. The English fishing fleet, which comprised 250 boats in 1626, when fighting between France and England once again broke out, was reduced to 40 within three years. This catastrophe led the English to override the traditional system of the fishers and establish a colony.

After several grants which failed, England gave Admiral David Kirke permission in 1637 to start a settlement and to exploit the fishing trade. He brought one hundred settlers to Ferryland, and developed a healthy depot, with a triangular trade between London, Boston, and Ferryland. When Oliver Cromwell came to power in the 1650s, he recalled Kirke to England. But in the meantime, settlement had begun. By 1655, about 500 settler-fishers lived along the English-held eastern coast.

The southern coast was "reserved" by the fleets from La Rochelle, St. Malo, Dieppe, and St.-Jean-de-Luz, which supplied fish to the Mediterranean area as well as to France. Reaping good profits, France was not inclined to make changes. Tentative French tries at colonization, which did not get a foothold until 1655, were only in response to English colonization on the eastern side of the island. The first effort was defeated by protests from St. Malo, the second by protests from The Hundred Associates, the third by a mutiny of the colony garrison. But each time, a few more settlers were placed. By 1664, Placentia had a population of 200. Thus did a few years of war end fishing traditions which had lasted for centuries.

The effect of the European wars inland, in what was then called New France, was less dramatic than in Acadia and New-foundland, but more frustrating and painful. After the occupation of Quebec by the English (1629–33), and Champlain's death (1635), France ignored its colony while fighting its battles at home. Settlers both broke the ground and held the forts without the aid of France, winning Canada with their sweat and blood. For the years 1633 to 1663, the crucial years of founding, were also bloody years of native war, as the Huron and the Iroquois fought for *la traite*.

The beaver is a non-migratory animal. It settles down in one place, lives in families, and does not reproduce itself quickly. Thus trappers rapidly depleted the beaver population in the areas they frequented. As the beaver were exterminated, the "beaver frontier" moved inland along the St. Lawrence, and the phenomenal increase in demand began drawing from the vast lands to the north and west, fanning out into the interior. The furs were traded from tribe to tribe; and the fur routes funneled into the Great Lakes region. From here they either went down the Ottawa and St. Lawrence to the French, or along the Hudson or Mohawk rivers to the Dutch and English. Which route they took depended on whether the entrepreneurs were Huron or Iroquois.

In 1640, the Dutch in New York began supplying firearms to the Iroquois, and during the next ten years the Iroquois' attacks on their competitors increased alarmingly. Till then, hostilities had mainly been limited to the ambush of canoes and flotillas. Now the Iroquois were amassing armies of 200 to 300 warriors. Not only were the French reluctant to trade firearms to the Huron, but their own supply of arms from France was woefully small.

On July 4, 1648, the Iroquois Confederacy launched a major offensive against the Huron, of whom there were some 12,000, living in thirty-two villages. The villages were burned, and the people scattered; a quarter of them were killed. At last, in 1653, the offensive overreached itself and was halted at the Sault Ste. Marie. In five years, the Huron nation had been wiped out.

In 1649, when the French began to feel the effects of the great Iroquoian offensive, then-Governor d'Ailleboust had sixty-eight soldiers from France—sixty-eight soldiers to cover three posts, each sixty miles apart. He did what he could in the circumstances: he formed a forty-soldier mobile unit, which tried to race between the beleaguered settlements.

D'Ailleboust also saved *la traite*. The Indian wars had cut off
the fur trade, so the Governor began sending out "volunteers" to
locate Indian flotillas beyond the Huron lands and guide them to
the St. Lawrence. In 1656, when a large flotilla of canoes from a
tribe west of the Huron, the Ottawas, came down the St.
Lawrence, it was clear that the "volunteer" system was paying
off. The two young Frenchmen who led the flotilla succeeded not
only in their mission of bringing the furs out, but also in opening
up the vast territory around Lake Huron and Lake Superior. This
gave New France access to trade, through the Ottawas, with tribes
even farther west, the Assiniboine and Sioux.

Then with the Huron destroyed, the Iroquois turned on the
French, killing between fifty and one hundred colonists a year
from 1658 to 1663.

During nearly three decades of Iroquois wars, France hardly
noticed her colony. Both colonizing and the fur trade administration were under The Hundred Associates. That left defense to the
French government. For this it supplied a handful of soldiers and
a series of mediocre Governors. The most promising leader, Governor d'Ailleboust, had the misfortune to administer during the
Huron catastrophe, and when his term expired in 1651, he was replaced.

The Governor who followed d'Ailleboust in 1651 was Jean
de Lauzon, a corrupt Company official whose first act as Governor was to disperse the forty-soldier mobile unit in order to raise
his own salary. His last act was to abscond with most of the reve-
nues from the first canoes of Ottawa furs. In between, he granted
himself and his family most of the land along the south shore of the
St. Lawrence, from Quebec to Montreal.

One wonders how New France survived these thirty years of
war, the squabbling and greed, not to mention the strangulation of
the fur trade and the Iroquois attacks. New France not only survived; it flourished. From a population of 250 in 1634, it increased to 2,500 by 1663. From a single village, Quebec, it grew

into three communities—Quebec, Trois Rivières, Montreal—all of them with cultivated land, and one of them a real town.

A large part of the credit for this must go to the Church. Europe was experiencing a strong religious revival among the nobility, and the French Catholic Church channeled a good deal of this fervor into financial support for New France. Montreal was basically a religious "gift." This great city-to-be began with the formation in France of the Society of Notre-Dame for the Conversion of the Savages, having as its purpose the establishment of a hospital on the Island of Montreal. How the Society came to pick such an unlikely location—a wilderness outpost in the dead center of Indian hostilities—is anyone's guess. But the Society was sure from the first exactly where it wanted the hospital to be built, and nothing, neither the pleas of officials nor the exorbitant price Lauzon charged for the island, could deter it. Perhaps the Society was indeed inspired, for it chose two of the strongest leaders in the history of New France to head the enterprise: Jeanne Mance and the Sieur de Maisonneuve. With seventy contract laborers, they arrived in 1641.

By the time of the Iroquois offensive, some forty artisans, soldiers, and farmers had been induced to settle Montreal by Maisonneuve's attractive conditions. Strategically the most vulnerable of the settlements, it nearly collapsed during the early 1650s. It was saved by the hospital fund, which Jeanne Mance used for arms. Left to its own resources, Montreal became independent of Quebec and soon competed for the fur trade.

Despite their financial gifts, their industry in learning native languages, and their simple courage, the Jesuits made little headway in their original purpose, that of converting the "savages." Thousands of Indian babies and dying adults had received rites, but instruction of adults yielded more hostility than piety. The Huron already had a highly developed religion. By 1639, after a tremendous effort in Huronia, with ten missionaries in the field, only eighty-two healthy Indians had been baptized. Ironically, the number of white youths who converted to Indian life outnumbered the willingly baptized Indians. So the Jesuit efforts in the field must be considered a net loss. On the foundation they laid, however, the Catholic Church remains to this day a powerful force among *Canadiens* (French-speaking Canadians). And on the foundation they literally laid, the cities of Quebec and Montreal still stand.

The *habitants,* meanwhile, found themselves defending and nurturing a fur trade from which they were getting no profits at all. Establishing settlers finally concocted a remarkable plan which they presented to The Hundred Associates. Backed by the powerful Jesuits, they proposed to take over the fur trade. In 1645, the Community of Habitants was formed. Composed of all heads of families, it was a tremendous step toward self-government for the colony.

Then in 1663, France made the momentous decision to bring New France directly under the French government. Louis XIV became the *seigneur* of New France, and its administration became part of the royal government. This move undoubtedly brought a sense of relief to many of the people involved with the colony; the royal father was once again taking responsibility for his "children." But in retrospect we can see that it was not all to the good.

The colony was facing many problems in 1663, the most serious, of course, being the guerrilla warfare waged by the Iroquois. *La traite* fluctuated wildly between feast and famine. The Hundred Associates was beset with legal and financial problems. Liquor traffic with the Indians flourished. The sister colony of Acadia had been in English hands for nearly a decade, La Tour having worked out his final deal. And Newfoundland, while still essentially an international ground, had over twice as many English settlers as French. Both the Dutch and the English wanted inland Canada for its fur trade. Indeed, New France faced many problems.

On the positive side, New France had come through the

thirty crucial years since its foundation on its own. The settlers, left by France to fend for themselves, had learned to survive in the new country. The fledgling self-government, based on democratic principles, which accompanied the formation of the Community of Habitants, was a result of this self-sufficiency.

There had been signs that the Iroquois Confederacy— exhausted from fighting the French and other Indians on all sides—was considering a serious peace. The news that Louis XIV was asserting himself in Canada made the Iroquois fear that this meant hordes of French settlers would claim Indian lands, however, and they ceased negotiations at once.

New France developed independence from France indirectly, too, because of the instability of the fur trade. Had *la traite* not been choked off during many of these years, had it flourished, Quebec might have become, economically, just a big trading post. When the trade did not provide the colonists a living, they turned to the land. They dug in and rooted. While commercial ties with France weakened, ties with their new land grew strong. At times, as in the La Tour affair, Quebec demonstrated that it thought quite independently of France. And as early as 1651, the people began referring to themselves, not as French, but as *Canadois,* or later, *Canadiens*.

Considering that New France took the first steps toward democratic self-rule a good century before the U.S. Declaration of Independence, that colony might well have been the first modern democracy. This chance for autonomy was cut short in 1663 by Louis XIV's edict. And it would be two centuries before *Canadiens* again spoke for themselves.

The city of Quebec as it is today. (*Canadian Department of External Affairs*)

Canada's Tree Line (north of which no trees can grow) is indicated by dots. Only one major road and two railroads serve the Arctic lands of the Yukon and the Northwest Territories. Residents of small settlements get about by dogsled, snowmobile, or airplane. *(Dianna Gilmore)*

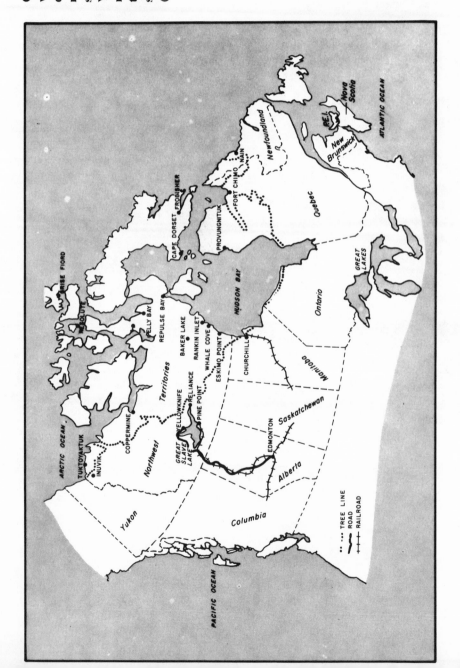

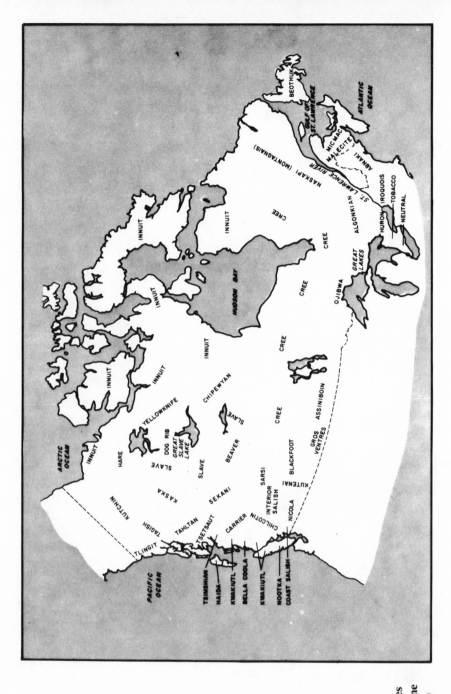

Location of the Native Peoples when the Europeans first came to Canada. (*Dianna Gilmore*)

Canadian geese in flight along the Lake Erie–Ontario shoreline. (*Canadian National Film Board*)

A gannet colony, one of half a dozen in Canada. (*Canadian Government Travel Bureau*)

Among Eskimo handicrafts is the making of lifelike masks such as this. (*Canadian National Film Board*)

Young men of the Six Nations perform traditional dances in Brantford, Ontario. (*Canadian National Film Board*)

An Eskimo mother adjusts her child's leather-and-fur legging. (*Canadian National Film Board*)

Caribou in the Yukon. (*Canadian National Film Board*)

A polar bear near Baffin Island, Northwest Territories. (*Canadian National Film Board*)

Canada's natural beauty features mountains (below, the Selwyns in the Yukon) and coastline (above, Nova Scotia). (*Canadian National Film Board*)

THE FRENCH TAKE ROOT

The Royal Regime, 1663 to 1763, began with France finally stepping in to claim its colony. It ended with that colony, New France, being lost to the English.

North America provided the great drama of the age during this century. Europe began to awaken to what was at stake. Not gold, not passage to the Orient, but land. Sheer land, with a vastness and diversity which had never been measured, and resources which could not be counted. And this was first made clear to the French King and his government by the tremendous profits in beaver pelts.

After the Huron nation was destroyed, the

beaver trade pushed west. The "beaver frontier" moved from Montreal to the Sault Ste. Marie—the piece of land where the three largest of the Great Lakes meet. The French began utilizing western tribes, such as the Assiniboine, Sioux, Cree, and Fox, to hunt beaver. The Ottawa who inhabited the crucial Sault area, and who were the best *canoteurs* (canoeists) on the continent, became the new go-betweens and transporters of the trade.

By the time Louis XIV began putting money and resources into Canada, the French traders had re-established a trading network. The only problem remaining was to get the furs to Montreal past the Iroquois. France finally sent 800 troops deep into Iroquois territory. The huge backlog of fur collected by the traders' new network around the Sault was free to move. And *la traite* began its age of rapid expansion.

The colonization policy for New France was a "compact colony policy." It called for containing expansion and concentrating settlers around the St. Lawrence. Viewed from the economic (beaver) and geographic (rivers) circumstances of New France, this policy was unrealistic. It was as though the United States government in Washington, two centuries later, had tried to restrict the gold-hungry '49ers to San Francisco. *La traite* required, not a thriving home colony, but hardly individual traders—*coureurs de bois*—who went out into the wilderness among the Indians. Newly arrived youths soon discovered that opportunities for adventure and good wages lay in taking to the woods and rivers. France poured "settlers" into one end of the St. Lawrence. Out the other end streamed *coureurs de bois*.

Unlike the English pioneers who "conquered" the environment and its Native Peoples, the *coureurs de bois* "infiltrated," adapting to the wilderness and to Indian life. Indian fundamentals were revolutionized by the enterprising French traders. From the intense knowledge which each tribe had of its own territory, *coureurs de bois* pieced together detailed maps of large areas of Canada. Likewise, the amazing *canot de maître* ("master canoe") was simply an enlargement of the Indian birch-bark canoe. From the light one-paddle boat of the Indians, the French traders developed craft as long as thirty-six feet, which required six paddlers and could carry six tons of pelts.

In a matter of a few years, the *coureurs de bois* had ceased to be the scouts that France envisioned them, scouts whose only business was to lead Indian canoes to Montreal and Quebec; now the *coureurs de bois* were primarily traders, and because the search for pelts led them deep into the wilderness, explorers—and because France tried to stop them, outlaws. This change can be seen in the career of one of the very first *coureurs de bois* who began as a scout.

One of the two young scouts who guided the first Ottawa canoes to Montreal was Médard Chouart, sieur des Groseilliers. He later joined forces with an adventurous relative, Pierre Esprit Radisson. They spent the next few years in unexplored wilderness around the Great Lakes, and enriched the fur coffers of Montreal and Quebec considerably. In the course of this, they observed the Shield country of the Crees to the north of the Great Lakes. It was this area that struck their imagination, both for the excellent quality of northern furs and for the access inland which the huge Hudson Bay provided.

Instead of seizing upon this vision, the government of New France levied fines against the two *coureurs de bois* for an unauthorized departure into the wilderness. Like the La Tours before him, des Groseilliers journeyed to France to plead his case—which, like the case of the La Tours, fell on deaf ears. At this point the two *coureurs de bois*, like the La Tours, turned to England.

In 1668, des Groseilliers's own ship, the *Nonsuch,* became the first expedition to establish an English post on Hudson Bay. When the ship returned to England the next year, its cargo of fur showed such enormous profits that a company was formed. This "Governor and Company of Adventurers of England Trading into

Hudson's Bay'' is the same Hudson's Bay Company which survives to this day.

The English method of collecting furs was different than that of the French. Instead of sending traders inland, the English established their posts at the mouths of the large rivers that drained the Shield into Hudson Bay and James Bay. For the couple of months each summer that the bays were free of ice, English ships brought supplies and items for barter. They returned to New England and England stuffed to the gills with prime northern pelts.

This method of collecting furs involved relatively little overhead, since supplies and items for barter could be brought in directly by sea. Furthermore, the Indians had learned the relative values of European goods. The day of glass beads was over. They wanted woolen blankets, copper kettles, and metal goods, and they had become experts at judging quality. French manufactures, particularly wool and kettles, were inferior to and more expensive than English goods. The result was that the English traders drained the fur-rich Shield lands as surely as the large rivers drained the Shield. New France, as a result, turned its energies south.

The first thrust of southern settlement came almost immediately on the heels of England's staking out the north. Governor Louis de Frontenac convinced Louis XIV that since Iroquois overtures to the Ottawa were beginning to endanger the southern fur trade, a fort should be built at Lake Ontario, two hundred miles of wilderness from Montreal. Fort Frontenac was built in 1673. That same year the French reached the great Mississippi River.

At this time, France held all the land north of the St. Lawrence (with the exception of Hudson Bay), from Labrador to the Great Lakes, and all of the Great Lakes region, from north of Lake Superior to the valley of the Ohio River in the south. West of the Lakes, and south of the Ohio Valley, the land was by and large unknown. Tales drifted back to Quebec of a great river to the southwest of the Lakes, and Governor Frontenac sent a small expedition, headed by Louis Jolliet and Father Jacques Marquette, to explore it. On June 17, 1673, the party entered a broad sweeping river, flowing strongly south, the Mississippi. They continued down the great river, from forest to plain to wooded hill, all the way to Arkansas country, where they turned back in July. The news they brought to Quebec delighted Frontenac, and he began building Fort Niagara to facilitate southern trade.

Ft. Niagara actually served a dual purpose, for the same year it began as a trading post, 1679, the first sailing ship began service on the Great Lakes. Its owner was a former Jesuit who had explored and traded on the Great Lakes for a decade, Robert La Salle. Arrogant, taciturn, visionary, young La Salle had fired Frontenac's imagination from the beginning.

With Frontenac's encouragement, La Salle left with an expedition for the Mississippi. The party consisted of twenty-three French and thirty-one Abenakis and Mohicans, including ten Indian women and three children. They set out in the dead of winter and had to drag their supplies and boats on sledges. In April 1682, the expedition reached the Gulf of Mexico, where La Salle claimed the land, the Louisiana Territory, for Louis XIV.

Louis XIV approved another Mississippi expedition to be led by La Salle. This one, consisting of 300 adventurers, was to enter the mouth of the Mississippi and sail north. The expedition, however, landed on Texas shores, rather than at the mouth of the Mississippi. Hundreds of miles out of their way, hampered by wilderness and hostile Indians, the party tried for two years to find the great river, and failed. La Salle's arrogance was essential to commanding a lost party of 300 adventurers and holding them together for two years, but it provoked deep bitterness. In 1687, he was killed in ambush by two of his men. Most of the party either joined Indian tribes or were killed by other tribes. Only five, including La Salle's brother, made it back to Quebec.

These Mississippi voyages opened the floodgates south—for the trappers, not the French government. For a decade after La

Salle's last voyage, France ignored the Mississippi and adhered to its policy of non-expansion. But when trappers and *coureurs de bois* heard of the great wealth of beaver in Ohio and Illinois, they streamed south. France, instead of following this wave of expansion, tried desperately to keep the traders in Montreal and Quebec. In 1681, for instance, the same year France issued only 25 official trading permits, an estimated 500 *coureurs de bois* headed for the wilds. France in its majestic splendor proclaimed regulations to restrict the traders. The Church with equal majesty proclaimed the excommunication of traffickers in brandy. In the wilderness of the New World, however, France and the Church seemed very far away.

All of the Governors were, in fact, active fur traders. One of them, Governor La Barre, sent a message to the Iroquois, telling them they could attack and rob any French *coureur de bois* who could not produce an official permit. He claimed he was trying to cut down on unauthorized traders. But the truth is that he subsidized many of the "unauthorized traders" himself and was trying to cut down on competition. In this case, justice was done. One of the first flotillas seized by the Iroquois, seven canoes containing 16,000 pounds of trade goods, belonged to the Governor himself.

Few Governors are worth mentioning because the colonial government is hardly worth mentioning. France made sure that neither commerce nor government in New France gained enough power to compete with the home country. France wanted the big profits securely based in France. The most enterprising individuals, such as La Tour and the founders of Hudson's Bay Company, were discouraged. The most "native" and independent French, such as the *coureurs de bois,* were punished if caught.

The wealthy fur merchants developed no native government, as did the fish and shipbuilding capitalists of Boston, because they were working for, or had strong ties with, even wealthier merchants back in France; many stayed in New France only for the length of time it took them to make a tidy fortune. There was no "national" feeling among the merchants of Montreal and Quebec; their profits and pleasures were French. And it is significant that the printing press, so important to the growing independence of the English colonies to the south, was completely absent from New France.

The class that France supposed to be the ruling class, the *seigneurs,* was nothing of the kind. Nominally the "landowners," they were hardly more influential than their "tenants." Canadian historian A. L. Burt notes that the wilderness democratized the people. "It was not uncommon for the lord of a manor, his lady, and his daughters to toil together in the fields. Such was the levelling influence of frontier life."

Louis XIV had envisioned New France as just another province, or *département,* of France. But the *département* was thousands of miles across the Atlantic Ocean. The only direct communication between ruler and ruled was by correspondence, carried by boat. It took months for a letter to reach French ministers; it took months for an answer to return. Legal quarrels took two or three years to resolve. Quarrels became battles, expediency became corruption.

Not only did the traders ignore the attempt to restrict them to the St. Lawrence; they soon discovered that English goods were cheaper and more desirable, that the English paid more for pelts, than the French. They began trading, first with the Iroquois, then directly with the English. Worse still, the plentiful beaver pelts from the Mississippi lands began to flood the market, and these were not the prime pelts of northern Canada.

The merchants in Quebec and Montreal were suddenly swamped with inferior southern pelts, and in turn they unloaded the "Illinois" beaver pelts on the entrepreneurs in France. The economics of the trade became so strained, the trading network so far-flung and the supply of beaver pelts so overwhelming, that even a tiny whim might topple the whole system. In 1696, the European fashion in men's hats changed. The market for beaver fur collapsed.

It was a trauma that nearly destroyed all French trade. The Indians who had become dependent on *la traite,* whether in transporting or bartering, were stranded. The 25 trading permits were revoked, and most of the western forts were closed. The Indians who had settled around these posts returned to their hunting. The wealthy merchants of Quebec packed their bags and returned home to France. It was the end of a magnificent, but highly unstable, era.

Unstable as the trade proved in the end, it provided the most dramatic exploration in North American history. La Salle had sailed all the way down the Mississippi, exploring the future United States down the middle, north to south. Less well remembered are the French traders who carried *la traite* as far northwest as the Saskatchewan River, halfway across the continent, and as far southwest as Spanish Taos and Santa Fe.

Meanwhile, the uncontrollable expansion of *la traite,* the weakness and corruption of the French colonial administration, and the lack of native government had left a vacuum. An unofficial government began to take shape through the Church. The first Bishop of Canada, François de Montmorency-Laval, served for twenty-five years, retiring in 1684. During this time Laval held tremendous power. A tireless and zealous supporter of the Jesuits, he was equally capable of manipulating support from the wealthy merchants. His one aim was to ensure that New France would be ruled by the Church. And the Church was destined to outlast both the French colonial government and *la traite.* For it was the only institution that spoke for the *habitants.*

Perhaps the most interesting aspect of the rise and fall of *la traite* is that, for all its furious activity and high-level competition, it really had little to do with the colony of New France itself. The colonizers were not *coureurs de bois* but *habitants.* The profits of the boom by and large bypassed them. So did the fur market crash.

Most *Canadiens'* involvement in the fur trade was limited to picking up a little extra cash by trapping in the winter season. Or perhaps a couple of the farmer's children had taken to the woods as *coureurs de bois*. The self-sufficient farmer could easily withstand the loss of that little extra cash. And as for the youthful *coureurs de bois*, their parents no doubt believed they were just as well off coming back home, keeping out of mischief, and lending a hand with the crops.

The number of *habitants* had increased remarkably, from 2,500 at the beginning of the Royal Regime (1663), to 6,700 by 1673. The little capital Quebec, with its proud, solid buildings, boasted 1,000 citizens. Because of the large families most *habitants* produced, the proportion of young people in the general population was high. Twenty Jesuit fathers and brothers taught one hundred boys in their school; eighteen Ursuline nuns were engaged in teaching girls. And outside Quebec, another school was established to teach agriculture and the trades.

The other settlements were now real towns. Montreal was just half the size of Quebec, but it had a larger share of the fur trade. Little Trois Rivières had 150 residents and 40 houses protected by a stockade.

By 1682, the year La Salle sailed down the Mississippi, the land under cultivation had doubled. New France now had a population of 10,000, of whom 7,000 were farmers. There were 94 horses, 291 head of cattle, 572 sheep, and 6,657 oxen—almost as many oxen as farmers. These farmers now formed the solid body of the colony and this was due to the only leader during this period who could really be called great, the first Intendant, Jean Talon.

At this time, the French government was represented in the colony by the Governor. Most Governors were too busy with their fur trade to be interested in anything more than occasional military maneuvers. The scant local government consisted of a Sovereign Council, most members of which were wealthy fur merchants. Since both Governor and Sovereign Council were preoccupied with fur profits, that left too much civil authority for the King's comfort in the hands of Bishop Laval.

He therefore created a third office, Intendant, which was directly responsible to the King. The Governor was to stick to military affairs, the Bishop to religious matters, and civil affairs were left to the Intendant. It never worked out that way, for only the first Intendant, Talon, was strong enough to maintain authority.

Champlain is the "founder" of Canada; Talon is the "colonizer." In his first year, more than 250 new farms were established, and livestock production increased dramatically. When Talon arrived in New France, for instance, there were no horses. He imported 80 stallions and mares and distributed them among the *habitants,* with the understanding that each *habitant* would in turn give a foal to someone else.

Encouraged by France and the Church alike, the natural increase among the *habitants* was almost as dramatic as the expansion of *la traite.* Cash bonuses were given to soldiers who settled and to newlyweds, while Talon nurtured the new, inexperienced farmers. Perhaps the most famous policy was Louis XIV's exportation of marriageable young Frenchwomen for wives. These were called *filles de roi*—"daughters of the King."

No doubt the new land required courage of these young women, most of them from orphanages or poor peasant families, most of them no older than sixteen. But in focusing on the *filles de roi,* historians often neglect to remind us that women were not new to Canada.

There were women on the first doomed expedition of de Roberval in 1542. Women tilled the fields of Acadia before Champlain founded Quebec. A widow ran the first real farm in New France; most farm women put their hand to the plow. Jeanne

Mance is as much founder of Montreal as Maisonneuve. The Ursuline nuns were just as active in educating youngsters as the Jesuits. For several centuries, women of Canada were in fact generally better educated than men.

Women from the aristocracy by and large built Quebec with their gifts to the Jesuits. Women accompanied La Salle down the Mississippi. And even in war, they often excelled. Stories are told of women alone in their fields, attacked by three or four armed Iroquois, who managed to send the warriors flying. Stories are told of teenaged girls successfully defending their parents' farms. And we remember the fierce defense of Saint John by La Tour's second wife.

And all these things—the manual labor which was a woman's lot as much as a man's, the fighting for survival in a wilderness, the nurturing of education and culture—were often accomplished along with raising seven to twelve children. Fifteen was not uncommon. The high birth rate their Church and society demanded was as rigorous as the demands of their new environment.

While New France's population was increasing at a rapid rate, and the outlines of theocratic government were forming, Acadia remained underdeveloped. There are two reasons. In Acadia, Indian tribes—especially Micmacs and Malecites in the Abenaki Confederation—still owned much of the land, and their territory was respected by the Acadians. The other factor was that Acadia was a sorely troubled spot.

Left untended by France, not yet reached by booming New England, but harassed by both, the Acadians were both isolated from Europe's subsidies and raked by Europe's quarrels. During the last half of the seventeenth century, Acadia, though more or less held by France, received little or no aid. When France first formulated its colonial policies for New France, it sent—almost as an afterthought—sixty settlers, half of them women, to Acadia. And then France ignored Acadia. Within a couple of years, the new settlers were so impoverished that Talon had to supply them from Quebec to prevent their starving. He even had to provide a French flag.

The French colony really had to depend on New England for its supplies, and most of the traders who opened primitive stores, or plied their wares door to door, were English. This was true even in times of war: one French commander fighting the English found it necessary to supply his garrison by ordering wheat from Boston. In the face of meager French military aid, the burden of keeping Acadia from falling to the English fell to the Acadians themselves—or more specifically to their Abenaki allies.

The farmers, meanwhile, went about their business with only occasional military interruptions from the outside. Most of the population had made farmlands from the marshes. On these they grew rich crops of wheat, rye, barley, hemp, flax, and all manner of fruit trees. Having no roads, they had little use for the horse, but they raised cattle, sheep, pigs, and oxen by the thousands. Like the Acadian Indians, they supplemented their diets with fish and their incomes with furs. Even during this turbulent half-century, the population increased from about 400 to nearly 2,000—and most of that was natural increase since France sent so few settlers.

So it was that French-speaking people struck roots in the New World as war and history swirled around them.

TWO POWERS AT WAR

The English colonies to the south, meanwhile, were past the rooting stage and had long since blossomed. Although Acadia had been settled before New England, by 1689 the English colonies had a population of 100,000—compared to 15,000 in all the Canadian colonies put together. This was partly because England encouraged immigration more than did France, and partly because the land south of the border was warmer, easier to farm. It was also due to the difference in land use and in attitude toward property.

Whereas New France and Acadia adopted a feudalistic *community* system, the English colonies developed under the new capitalist concept of *pri-*

vate ownership. In the English colonies, land speculation was both very profitable for individuals and very efficient in promoting settlement. Boston merchants gained power and wealth from cod fishing; the landowners of Virginia and Pennsylvania gained power and wealth through the resale of land, that is, they bought large parcels of land and sold it off piecemeal to land-hungry immigrants. When the settlers arrived at their new homestead, they often found that not only was it in the middle of nowhere, far from civilization, but that Indians were under the impression that they owned the same piece of land.

The speculators solved this quandary by raising the cry against "the savages." While the white settlers and Indians fought to the death, the speculators counted their profits.

Some tribes fought fiercely, of course, and succeeded for a time in holding off the "progress of civilization." Most of them were defeated and massacred in the end. The Abenakis of Acadia are one exception. After sending several unsuccessful expeditions against the Abenakis, the English finally had to come to terms and recognize Indian territory. But the major exception was the Iroquois. The English learned early to respect this Confederacy and woo it as an ally.

During this time of peace, the Iroquois concentrated mainly on the smuggling trade between *coureurs de bois*, other Indians, merchants in Montreal, and the English colonies. By the 1680s, these smuggled furs accounted for a full quarter of the pelts from French territory. The Iroquois were so successful as entrepreneurs that they had no need for warfare, and they began to respond to France's offers of peace. They might not have taken up the hatchet again, but the French foolishly betrayed some of their warriors during a peace talk. This led to an Iroquois attack on the little village of Lachine, in which the inhabitants were massacred. The result was an all-out war between the Iroquois and the French.

When another European war erupted the same year, the

American hostilities spread into New England, and both the French and English kept up a steady stream of attacks on each other's settlements. As yet this warfare was still primarily a result of European politics. But now Europeans and Americans alike were beginning to see what was at stake. The prize was a whole continent, and the conflicts were becoming increasingly American in nature and origin.

The wars that lost Canada to France span about seventy years. The first set lasted from 1689 to 1713, at the end of which New France lost its outposts of Acadia, Newfoundland, and Hudson Bay. Then there was a generation of peace. The second set began in 1744, and at the end, in 1760, all French lands east of the Mississippi (except two small islands) were left to Britain and Spain. New France was no more.

During the first set, there were two major wars, called in Europe and Canada the War of the Grand Alliance and the War of the Spanish Succession. In the United States, these are called King William's War and Queen Anne's War. Essentially they were fought because Louis XIV of France was now the most powerful ruler in Europe, with ambitions of becoming even more powerful, and other European monarchs wanted to curb his power.

Louis XIV could muster tremendous force. But unlike England, France had several land borders to defend all at once against other European nations, and the long continuous years of war were costly. By 1713, France—though neither defeated decisively nor humbled—needed peace badly. In order to obtain it, Louis gave up the Canadian outposts of Acadia, Newfoundland, and Hudson Bay.

These European political terms were not a fair measure of the outcome of the wars in America, where in fact New France was essentially victorious. Considering that 15,000 people of New France were pitted against a population of 100,000 in the English colonies, New France showed itself very well in the field.

With the Iroquois attack on Lachine in 1689, the now-retired Governor Frontenac was quickly sent back to Canada. The following year, he led a massacre of the people of Schenectady, New York, and within the next few years he devastated the Iroquois, first the Mohawks and then the Onondagas and Oneidas. He continued to lead terrorist raids on New England, until the English colonies began pulling back within their frontiers. Frontenac was so successful militarily that the Iroquois negotiated peace in 1701, and they more or less withdrew from hostilities with France for forty years.

The turn of the century saw the English begin to return the fight. A powerful merchant named Samuel Vetch produced a plan, called the Albany Plan, for the invasion of Canada. Deeply involved in the Acadia trade, he urged the English to conquer Acadia and New France, both by sea and by land. Three costly attempts to do so were handled so inefficiently, however, that the British forces either dispersed or retreated. During the last attempt, in 1711, the two commanders of the expedition managed to wreck ten of their ships on Egg Island. When European hostilities were ended by the Treaty of Utrecht in 1713, France's loss of the Canadian outposts was really a result of the European part of the war, rather than of an English victory in North America.

For a generation, thirty years, there was peace. The Canadian people, having claimed every acre of their land with blood and toil, now prospered and increased. There were several distinct modes of life, not counting the colorful *coureurs de bois*.

Most of the *habitants* lived on farms or in rural communities, and they developed a characteristic style of dress. The men wore long trousers, large woolen coats, moccasins, and a soft cap with a long peak, called a *tuque*—a blue *tuque* if one lived near Montreal, a red one if near Quebec. And in his leisure hours, the man often smoked a long-stemmed pipe of Canadian tobacco. The farming woman wore shorter, more practical skirts than her city cousin. For special occasions, she wore a white cap and colored bodice, and sometimes indulged herself in French shoes, though practical moccasins were more usual for every day. Both sexes often played cards to pass the time through the long winter, and there were of course skating and sleighing parties on the St. Lawrence River.

The townspeople of Quebec imitated France, as much as distance and communications would permit, in their dress and pleasures. Wealthy officials and merchants offered lavish dinner parties (often on money from the public coffers), and their ladies indulged in genteel salons and flirtations.

Montreal, on the other hand, was more of a frontier town, with less time for fashion. Its leading merchants and legions of minor traders usually dressed in frontier or Indian styles which were simple and practical. And Montreal attracted the more serious women in the tradition of Jeanne Mance—women such as Marguerite Bourgeoys who founded schools for girls in Montreal and six nearby communities, and Madame de Repentigny who set up the first weavers' workshop to produce Canadian cloth.

Acadians, too, had developed a distinctive culture, based on leisurely pastoral farming in their fertile, mild land. They tended sheep and cattle, traded for manufactures with New Englanders, farmed their lands, and hunted and fished when it pleased them. Their daughters and sons left Port Royal to break new land and build new communities, flowing northeast into future Nova Scotia. The Acadian population increased during this peace from under 2,000 in 1713 to over 10,000 in 1744. Their English "masters" amounted to a puny garrison or two, and as for the New England traders who constantly plied their coasts, the Acadians had always welcomed them.

The English did confront the Acadians with a thorny problem. Uneasy with such a large French-speaking population as "subjects," the English required an oath of allegiance to Britain. The Acadians, who had seen French and English governments push each other out of Acadia many times, were not about to pledge to take up arms against France. And furthermore, their own Catholic clergy, along with their allies the Abenakis, were fanatically opposed to the Protestant British. It was not unusual for priests to lead the Indians in attacking English settlements. Among themselves, the Acadian farmers decided that their best course was to stay neutral. They offered to swear that they would bear arms against *neither* side. Met with this stiff resistance, the British finally granted the Acadians neutral status.

This was peace in America, but it was an armed peace. Now without Acadia to guard the entrance to the St. Lawrence, the French began building a massive fort on Cape Breton Island, called Louisbourg. The British likewise went to considerable expense to construct a gigantic fort at Churchill on Hudson Bay, which took forty years to complete. Not that it mattered much. Both Louisbourg and Churchill fell when put to the test.

The hostilities once again began as a European war, the War of the Austrian Succession (called King George's War in the United States) in 1744. Louisbourg was attacked by a large and highly efficient force from New England. Not well situated in terms of its terrain, it fell after seven weeks of heavy shelling, but it held out long enough to prevent the British from making their way up the St. Lawrence before winter closed in. The French attacked Annapolis Royal (formerly Port Royal) in Acadia. Then the hostilities petered out. European peace was signed in 1748—but it was not really peace.

France had now firmly established itself in the Ohio and Louisiana territories. The British, however, had prospered and increased even more than the French, and by the middle of the eighteenth century, British settlers finally crossed the great barrier of the Appalachians, spilling into the Ohio Valley. With flimsy justification, the English granted this whole territory to the Virginia and Maryland Ohio Company—a company of hastily assembled Virginia land speculators, including a young landowner named George Washington. The Ohio Company began selling

France's land to settlers and sending in traders. France completely reversed its "compact colony" policy and built a chain of forts down the Mississippi. Completed by 1753, they effectively stopped the British.

It was at this point that the young and inexperienced George Washington appeared with 160 armed Virginians to secure his interests. He came upon a detachment of 30 French soldiers and, although France and Britain were not at war, he led a surprise attack on their camp, killing ten and capturing the rest.

Expecting reprisal, Washington immediately built Fort Necessity. When the French appeared they numbered 700 soldiers against Washington's 350, but Washington had the advantage of a nine-gun fort. In one day's battle, Washington lost 80 soldiers, the Canadians three. He led such a speedy retreat that his followers left two flags behind.

This was really the opening battle of the Seven Years' War (called the French and Indian War in the United States). Although France and England did not formally declare war until 1756, two years later, hostilities on American soil increased.

In Acadia, meanwhile, the British were as busy securing their position as the French were in the heartland. Halifax was established in what was now called Nova Scotia, and by 1753, had 4,200 inhabitants. Now it seemed possible to establish a thoroughly English colony without need of the Acadians.

Despite the fact that through the War of the Austrian Succession the Acadians had remained loyal to their pledge of neutrality, the British demanded a loyalty oath again. The Acadians once again firmly refused, citing Britain's official recognition of their neutral status. This time the English used the refusal as an excuse to take the Acadians' land.

Soldiers dragged whole families from their farmhouses, burned their farms, confiscated their livestock, and marched the unfortunate prisoners to stockades. The Acadians were not given the option to emigrate to nearby French territory. Instead they were boarded on tightly packed ships and dispersed among the English colonies all along the Atlantic coast. Families were separated and transported according to age and sex. All the young men, for instance, were shipped first, because they were potential warriors. And when the young men protestèd, pleading to be kept with their parents or wives or children or sweethearts, they were marched on ship at the point of bayonets. Some of the Acadians had sensed danger and emigrated in time. Some escaped to the woods ahead of the soldiers. One group seized the ship on which they were boarded, and sailed it back home. But all in all, between 6,000 and 7,000 people were exiled.

As for the English colonies on the Atlantic, they were none too happy about receiving "enemies" into their midst, and none too happy about the expense of providing for the exiles. But once the Acadians arrived, the common bond between one struggling colonist and another smoothed the relationship. The English colonists, though imposed upon, resolved to behave in a "Christian" manner. The exiles were allowed to go into trades. If they took to the woods heading for home, the English colonists looked the other way. The colony in Georgia actually allowed the displaced persons to build large ships for themselves and sail home. Within eight years, 2,600 Acadians were back farming their land in Acadia. But by then the war was over.

By the time France and Britain formally declared war in 1756, the American hostilities had been going on for two years, and the Acadians had been deported. For the first few years, the British fared badly, both in Europe and in America. Then in late 1757, the daring statesman William Pitt gained the support of his frightened King and Cabinet for a remarkable plan. Leave Britain's allies to fight the battle in Europe, he urged. Let us attack France on the colonial level. And so the full military might of England was brought to bear on the small, struggling settlements of New France.

When we compare the human resources of the French and

British colonies, the imbalance is astonishing. The British-Americans numbered over a million, the French 70,000. Likewise, 28,000 British troops were pitted against the 6,000 French at Louisbourg. Inland, around Lake Champlain, south of Montreal, 15,000 soldiers were sent against less than 4,000 French. The outcome was predictable. The question was not who would win, but why the victory took two years from the time Pitt's overwhelming force set sail from England. Seldom can such a question be answered with the name of one individual, but in this case, it can: the Marquis de Montcalm.

A small, witty, highly educated man, he led some of the most brilliant actions in the history of America. He managed to muster his sparse troops from France, and to unite them firmly with the native *Canadien* soldiers and allied Indians. This was not easy: the French and *Canadiens* had different modes of fighting, the one on open ground, the other in small guerrilla bands, "Indian-style." And the Indians, of course, tended to be independent of white leadership. Yet Montcalm managed to keep a firm hand with his odd army, to stifle the French soldiers' disdain of the *Canadiens,* and to command loyalty from the rough *Canadiens,* without any imposition of the severe punishments to which lesser leaders resort. His defense of inland Canada against such overwhelming odds was so effective in thwarting the British that they had to revise their plans and turn their main attack on Louisbourg.

Once again Louisbourg held out, this time for six weeks under heavy shelling, but this time it did not save Quebec. In June 1759, the huge British navy and army moved up the unprotected St. Lawrence and reached Quebec. In command was General James Wolfe, who had led the attack on Louisbourg. Now faced with the little capital, Wolfe was stunned. This was no Louisbourg, built with no thought of terrain. No, this was the city of Champlain. Perched on an awesome bluff, it was unassailable.

For weeks, Wolfe sailed back and forth, stymied. He ravaged the countryside, burning farms and killing *habitants,* and he made several attempts to gain a foothold. These were all met by Montcalm with brilliant tactics in clash after clash. It was now September, and Wolfe became desperate to fight a decisive action before winter. At last he found a tiny trail leading to the top of the bluff.

He led his soldiers up at nightfall. Challenged by the sentries, they were saved by the quick wit of a Scots Highlander who responded in perfect French. And when Quebec awoke the next morning, the British army was assembled on the Plains of Abraham outside the city gates.

Montcalm, perhaps under as much tension as Wolfe and certainly worried about letting the British entrench themselves, made the mistake of joining battle on the open field. The battle was brief, a disastrous rout for the French, and both Montcalm and Wolfe were killed.

French forces from Montreal attacked the British at Quebec the next spring, and won. But they did not have the artillery required to take the city itself, and the two forces remained in a stalemate, waiting to see whether it was the French or the British who first sailed up the St. Lawrence come May. The tide having turned in Europe, it was the British.

They pursued the French back to Montreal upon which the English forces hastened to converge. Montreal surrendered in September 1760. The war continued in Europe for a couple of years longer. Then by the Treaty of Paris in 1763, all French territory east of the Mississippi (except the tiny islands of St. Pierre and Miquelon, which France retained, and New Orleans, which was turned over to Spain) was ceded to Britain.

The process by which France lost Canada was a long one, a process built into the very relationship between France and its colony. Economists might blame the loss on the unstable beaver trade. Or they might say that France's economy was geared to waging war in Europe rather than settling American colonies. Militarists might say that England and New England supplied a greater number of soldiers. Politicians might conclude that

New France had had no opportunity to organize its own government, and that the one supplied by France was weak and corrupt.

In any case, New France fell to the British; that was what
mattered then. What matters now is what has happened since.

FINDING COMMON GROUND

SEVEN

By the time of the Conquest, the institutions of New France were represented by several hundred wealthy merchants, landed nobles, French government officials, and members of the Church hierarchy. Their society imitated that of Paris insofar as it was possible.

The real identity of Canada, however, was represented by some 60,000 *habitants*. Often deserted by France and forced to rely on their own resources, the *habitants* adapted to the land and developed their own culture. The *Canadiens* seldom participated in the society of pseudo-Parisians, and felt its presence only when taxes or tithes were imposed. They found they had little in common with leaders whose culture was borrowed, whose manners were artificial, whose government was corrupt. The Conquest meant that the pseudo-French institutions vanished, as the nobles, merchants, officials, and Church hierarchy fled back to France. They left behind a sturdy, thriving people, the *Canadiens,* who were soon joined by another thriving people—the *Anglais.*

After driving French institutions from Canada, the *Anglais*— as the French Canadians called the English conquerors—replaced them with their own. This is to say, the British took over the fur commerce in Montreal. It was the English-speaking merchants who came to control the economy of Canada. As the world became increasingly industrialized, this fact would become very important indeed. For the time being, it mattered little to the French Canadians, who wanted only to farm and be left alone.

English institutions, however, also included the Anglican Church, the English language, and the township system of dividing land. These could not be imposed on a French-speaking Catholic people, who already had their farms laid out in waterfront strips. The conquerors had a perplexing problem: the fur trade was secured by British merchants, but what to do with the 60,000 French Canadians who surrounded them?

The new merchants in Montreal clamored for "representative government" and English laws. Since by law in England, Roman Catholics were excluded from the rights of citizenship, voting, and office-holding, "representative government" would have meant a handful of English merchants ruling 60,000 *Canadiens.* Fortunately, the first two Governors were military officers with great respect for the *habitant* and little liking for the merchant. The first, General James Murray, was recalled because of the merchants' fury. His replacement was Guy Carleton, who was even more firm about leaving the *Canadiens* to themselves.

Carleton soon perceived that the *habitants* feared, not the loss of the fur trade—it had never really been theirs anyway—but the loss of their culture. They wanted to keep their language, land, and religion, and to be left alone. Carleton turned to the *habitants'* spokesmen, the priests, for advice.

Bishop Laval, in welding the Church to *Canadien* identity, had started the effective system of training *habitant* boys to be parish priests rather than importing priests from France. Thus, the lower-status priests were from *habitant* families and were therefore trusted by the *Canadiens*. Despite the departure of the Church hierarchy (a temporary departure, as it turned out), the priests still maintained a solid parish organizaiton.

Carleton consulted with the priests and then presented Canada with the Quebec Act of 1774, guaranteeing freedom of language and religion, and re-establishing French civil law and land tenancy. The Act passed through the British Parliament quite easily. England was eager to establish good relations with its new *Canadien* colony, for it was having serious troubles with its British colonies to the south.

The Seven Years' (or French and Indian) War that won New France left ill feeling between Britain and its thirteen colonies to the south. It had been a costly war, for Britain had thrown all of its military might into conquering New France. From Britain's point of view, the colonies should have been made to pay for the war; after all, it had been waged in their own "defense." The colonies, on the other hand, felt that if Britain claimed to own their territory, and if Britain reaped the major profits from their natural resources, then Britain ought to foot the bill for increasing its empire. To bring its colonies to heel, Britain first imposed the Stamp Act and the Tea Tax. Then it imposed the Quebec Act.

The Quebec Act was a brilliant proposal. In ensured the loyalty of the French Canadians by preserving their culture. And it ensured the loyalty of the *Anglais* merchants by extending the boundaries of the colony (all called Quebec at this time) to include the whole Ohio-Mississippi territory and its fur trade. This did not sit well with the large Virginia land speculators, who had fought the Seven Years' War mainly to gain access to this territory. As angry as the Bostonians were about the Tea Tax, the Virginians were angrier still about the Quebec Act of 1774.

The suddenness of the American Revolution took the colonies by surprise. Distinctions between Loyalist and Revolutionary were not clear; by John Adams' own estimate, one-third of the colonial population were Loyalist sympathizers. The split when it came was violent and bitter. Many Americans, Tory and Revolutionary alike, were driven from their homes, tarred and feathered, ridiculed by the very people they thought friends and neighbors. The wound was a long time healing.

The French Canadians more or less stayed out of the war, disappointing both sides. One of the first acts of the Continental Congress in 1774 was to invite Quebec and Nova Scotia to join the colonies, for they were "the only link wanting to complete the bright and strong chain of Union."

There was no response, so the Continental Army resorted to force. In the fall of 1775, General Richard Montgomery took Montreal and marched on to Quebec. There he was joined by General Benedict Arnold, who had led 1,100 armed patriots (of whom only 650 made it) on an incredible journey through the Maine wilderness, during winter, to reach Montgomery. Outside the walls of Quebec, they were stopped.

This military mission was followed by a high-powered diplomatic mission, led by Benjamin Franklin. It included Fleury Mesplet, who immediately established himself with his French-speaking compatriots in Montreal and became the first Canadian printer. But Franklin himself failed to win the *Canadiens'* confidence.

The British had as little success with the *Canadiens* as had the Colonists. A few hundred *Canadiens* joined the British troops, but most of the sturdy *habitants* ignored the war. Guy Carleton, who had championed their culture and pushed the Quebec Act in some hopes of winning their loyalty, observed sadly, "I think there is nothing to fear from them while we are in a state of prosperity, and nothing to hope for when in distress."

Meanwhile, large numbers of Tories flocked into Canada. Calling themselves United Empire, or U.E., Loyalists, they came with a special bitterness toward the United States and a compulsion toward all things British. Acadia was now divided roughly between New Brunswick and Nova Scotia. Here the U.E. Loyalists came first, and took over the diked farmlands left by the Acadians. They developed the West Indies trade and started timber and shipbuilding industries. By the time the American Revolution was over, they numbered 20,000, as compared to less than 3,000 returned Acadians.

Of the Loyalists who went to Quebec, some took over the large *seigneuries* which had been deserted by rich French landowners—especially along the south shore of the St. Lawrence, in what became known as the Eastern Townships of Quebec. Others moved into the unsettled Great Lakes territory where once the Huron and Ottawa had dominated, and broke new land for farms. To compensate these Loyalists for land lost in the United States, England granted large tracts, or sold them at very low prices, and furnished settlers with food and implements to get started.

These terms attracted more settlers from the United States, even settlers who were not U.E. Loyalists and Anglican, but small farmers, often Methodist, who simply wanted good land. They brought with them U.S. culture, typically U.S. speech, and such U.S. holidays as Thanksgiving.

Further balancing the influence of the U.E. Loyalists were the considerable number of Scots, some of them Catholic but most of them Presbyterian, who emigrated early from the Scottish Highlands. Soon the very British U.E. Loyalists were only a small part of the total British population.

By the time peace was declared in 1783, Quebec was a different land. From an almost totally French-speaking population, with a sprinkling of British merchants and officials, the huge colony was well on its way to having a half-English-speaking, half-French-speaking population. The Great Lakes region had become an area culturally distinct from the St. Lawrence region, an area of plain English-speaking farmers, many of them from the United States, with democratic ideas. They pushed for representative government.

Unable to reconcile two so different cultures, the British decided to split them up. So it was that, by the Constitutional Act (Canada Act) of 1791, the huge province of Quebec was split into two parts, named Upper Canada in the Great Lakes area, and Lower Canada along the St. Lawrence.

The American Revolution was a turning point for the Native Peoples of America as well as for Canadian settlers. As soon as new lands were discovered, they were staked out, either by the British or by the burgeoning United States. Settlers were breaking land at a fast pace, and explorers were reaching all but the most inaccessible corners of the continent. The consequences for the Native Peoples were severe.

The Beothuk were annihilated. Unlike other Canadians, Newfoundland fishers had never been dependent on the Indians for survival or business, and so had little respect for them. They generally regarded the Beothuk as pests and savages, and killed them as a sport, in hunting parties. The last known Beothuk, Nancy Shawanahdit, died in captivity in 1829.

The Montagnais and Naskapi of Labrador were more fortunate. They continued to trade and trap, and were pretty much left alone, mainly because the land they inhabited was not considered worth the settlers' trouble. The Micmac of Nova Scotia became dependent on the new white culture, but they managed to make a good enough living, trading with and transporting goods to the number of little coastal villages that sprang up. They lived in small camps separate from the settlers, and for many years were free to roam the unsettled interior. But in general, all over the continent at this time, there was a violent clash between Indian culture and white civilization.

In Canada, the Native Peoples fared somewhat better than in

the United States, perhaps because in early years the settlers were dependent on good Indian relations for survival and for continuance of the fur trade. Later, the British government regarded the Indians as a useful buffer between British North America—that is, the Canadian colonies—and the ever-expanding population of the United States. For whatever reason, Canada had a long tradition of trying to come to terms with, rather than crush, the Indians.

The thrust of white civilization into Indian frontiers at this time came from the southeast, that is, from the United States. The Indians in Central Canada tended to attack south of the border and withdraw north of it. After the French lost the Seven Years' War, for instance, the Ottawas under Pontiac retook almost every fort in the Ohio Valley before coming to terms with the British. Most Iroquois, who had remained Loyalist, had (with the exception of the Senecas) moved to Canada. Their spokesman, the Mohawk Chief Joseph Brant, organized Indians of many different tribes against the U.S. army. They were at last decisively defeated at Fallen Timbers in 1794. Another Indian nationalist, Tecumseh, who preached that no one *owns* the land, that all land belongs to all people, and that all Indians have a common enemy, eventually amassed an army of 3,000 which joined the British during the War of 1812. All of these great leaders had their base in Canada.

The most dramatic incident on Canadian soil, on the Plains, was only a matter of a few paltry skirmishes compared to these great dramas. But this incident is still important, for it introduced Canada to the Plains, the Métis, and a conflict that was to last for the better part of a century.

Around the Red River area near the eastern edge of the Plains, the Cree Indians had mingled with the *coureurs de bois* and with the French and Scots fur traders. Their half-breed children built their own settlements on the Red River and formed a new nation: the Métis. The economy of both the Cree and Métis was based on trading, transporting, producing pemmican (the Indian mixture of pounded meat and berries) in huge bales to supply the burgeoning exploration and trade in the northwest, and hunting buffalo.

In 1811, the Earl of Selkirk convinced the Hudson's Bay Company to turn over some of their Plains territory to him. He moved settlers into the Red River area and surveyed a good chunk of territory. His agent began to confiscate some of the bales of pemmican. The Métis and Crees started to harass the settlement, and kept it up long enough to ruin Selkirk's large-scale plans. But the settlement was there to stay, and the Métis and the Hudson's Bay Company hastened to settle their differences for the time being. This led to the first Canadian-Indian treaty, the Selkirk Treaty of 1817. It was a century of expansion, and there was more than enough room for everyone on the frontier.

By the end of the eighteenth century, the outlines of future Canada were apparent. Explorers had reached the Rockies and the Arctic. And just about this time, the Russians, with a Danish explorer named Bering, reached America from Asia. When word of this leaked out, England sent their great navigator, Captain James Cook, to this area. He mapped the northern Pacific Coast extensively and even sailed through the Bering Strait as far as the polar ice pack in 1778.

Meanwhile, merchants in Montreal had picked up the strands of the old French fur trade, employing the *coureurs de bois* who had stayed in the wilderness after the Conquest. In 1779, the Montreal merchants united under the North West Company. Rough, stubborn, and daring, the Nor'Westers were said to be more at home in a canoe than on land. Aggressive Scots and *Canadien* traders now furiously competed with the Hudson's Bay Company for the rich furs of the Northwest interior. This competition led to a bitter war, in which the traders of the two companies had no hesitation about murdering one another.

With the discovery of the Pacific Coast, the Nor'Westers determined to reach the ocean by land, ahead of the Hudson's Bay people. In 1787, the Montreal company sent out a Scot, Alexander Mackenzie. From what neighboring Indians told him, he hoped the Peace River would lead him through the Rockies. In 1793, in a specially built canoe, Mackenzie followed the mighty river through its treacherous canyons to the intermountain plateau. Then he found an Indian trail which led from the plateau, through the Coast Range, to the lush Pacific slope. And there was the Pacific Ocean. Alexander Mackenzie became the first recorded person to cross the entire continent, from sea to sea.

Although the Nor'Westers won the race for the Pacific Coast, they lost the financial war. It was the cautious Hudson's Bay Company that emerged successful from the vicious competition between the two great companies. It was a bitter defeat, for the Nor'Westers had won the Pacific Coast race by means of stubborn courage; it was the North West Company financiers in Montreal, not they, who had been lacking. The two companies merged in 1821. By their earlier competition, however, they had added the Pacific Coast of British Columbia to future Canada.

By the end of the eighteenth century, seven different British North American colonies were forming their own separate characters and governments. Farthest west was the Pacific Coast, not technically yet a colony, but developing colonial institutions under the ownership of the Hudson's Bay Company. This was especially true after 1846, when the United States and England agreed on the boundary between Oregon and British Columbia. Likewise, Lower and Upper Canada each had its distinct character, economy, and needs. And in the Maritimes alone were three distinct colonies—New Brunswick, Nova Scotia, and Prince Edward Island. And then there was Newfoundland. Each of these areas made its own journey toward independence, first in achieving separate colonial status, then in achieving its own representative government.

New Brunswick was carved out of Nova Scotia (formerly Acadia) and Maine in 1784. A vast timber reserve, its forests were soon filled with rough lumber camps, and its economy geared to the drastic fluctuations resulting from the timber boom. Fortunes were made out of dramatic logging drives down the rivers to the sea. Fortunes, and the lives of many lumberjacks, were lost when those logs got caught in a "jam," and piled up like matchsticks along the way.

The American Revolution brought a large number of U.E. Loyalists to New Brunswick, and there were significant immigrations of Scots and Irish. Most of these—Loyalist and immigrant alike, Anglican and Methodist or Catholic alike—were poor farmers preoccupied with clearing modest farms from the wilderness. But one group of wealthy U.E. Loyalists established themselves in Saint John, New Brunswick, and soon after U.S. independence succeeded in taking command of the colony. This small group preached that loyalty to God and the King demanded submission on the part of the populace. And since the small farmers and poor lumberjacks were isolated in the forests and on the farms, the "populace" had little opportunity to question this government.

The Church of England, or Anglican Church, was the only sanctioned faith in New Brunswick. Roman Catholics (who included many Irish and Scots, and virtually all Acadians) could not vote until 1810, and the marriages of dissenting non-Anglican Protestants were not legal until 1832. Education was available only to the sons of "Anglican gentlemen." Because of anti-United States sentiment, these men who set themselves up as petty colonial aristocrats were able to keep control of the government.

Prince Edward Island (PEI) became a colony separate from Nova Scotia even earlier than New Brunswick, in 1769. Indeed, little PEI became the most distinct colony of all. Mild of climate, with fertile farmland, it proved ideal for produce farming and developed as the "garden" of the Maritimes. Its residents traded only with neighboring colonies, growing self-sufficient and insular. They cared little about world—or even Maritime—politics.

After the exile of the Acadians, PEI was parceled out, as

compensation and reward, to a few wealthy Loyalists and retired officers, many of whom did not even live on the island. Charlotte-town was the center of an "aristocracy" similar to that of Saint John, and as in New Brunswick, all religions except the Anglican Church suffered discrimination. The small farmers who actually worked the land could not get clear title to their farms, and the conflict between absentee landlord and resident tenant kept PEI politics in constant turmoil. In 1818, an autocratic Governor or-dered the elected Assembly arrested. Only one member managed to escape. He was smuggled aboard a ship in a cask, and finally reached London with the islanders' petition. The tiny, fiercely in-dependent island was becoming a headache to Great Britain.

Nova Scotia was the largest and most exciting of the Mari-time colonies. Immigrants from the United States (including sev-eral thousand blacks), Scotland, England, and Germany formed little settlements and mingled in the economic life of the colony. Shipbuilding was in its heyday, as was the trade with the West Indies. By 1850, Nova Scotians were shipping a fourth of the world's goods.

Although the financial oligarchy in Halifax "owned" Nova Scotia, just as Saint John "owned" New Brunswick and Char-lottetown "owned" PEI, dozens of little coastal settlements and farming communities prospered in their own right. Because of their intense contact with the outside world, Nova Scotians were more cosmopolitan than their Maritime neighbors. While New Brunswick and PEI struggled to establish elementary education, Nova Scotia was already building libraries and universities, churn-ing out dozens of newspapers, establishing self-help societies in agriculture and mechanics. By the early 1800s, Nova Scotians had so much independence and sense of community that representative government was only a matter of time.

Newfoundland as usual was a case unto itself. England re-sisted granting it even colonial status, for Newfoundland was con-sidered, not a "land," but according to Britain, a "great ship moored near the banks during the fishing season, for the convenience of English fishermen.'' The voices the British Parliament heard were those of the English merchants who controlled the trans-Atlantic fisheries, and the admirals of the British navy, who trained their new officers on the fishing fleets.

But the trans-Atlantic fisheries were fighting a losing battle. By the early 1800s, permanent Newfoundlanders numbered 60,000. St. John's was a port city of 12,000, half of whom were Roman Catholics, and the other half Anglicans, Presbyterians, and Methodists. The rest of the settlers were scattered along the coasts in tiny "outports." They lived by cod fishing in the summer and sealing in the winter. Because the English fleets left for the winter, the Newfoundlanders accounted for virtually all of the sealing catch. And because their system of drying cod on shore proved much more efficient than trans-Atlantic fishing, they soon came to account for almost all of the cod catch. The trans-Atlantic fisheries were obsolete. But the system of non-government that protected them continued to be imposed by Britain until 1824.

Nevertheless Britain's attitude toward its colonies was beginning to change. During the early 1700s, Britain had looked upon its overseas possessions as suppliers of raw resources, in which any sign of independence or self-government was a threat. During the late 1700s, the growing independence of the colonies coincided with a change in mood by Great Britain. Free trade and free competition were popular concepts; the British public and their lawmakers began to see the old colonial system, and its system of dependence and privilege, as being outmoded. The colonies and their eternal problems were becoming a nuisance. Great Britain was inclined to let them stand on their own feet.

One of the first concessions England made to colonial realities, in the case of each colony, was the establishment of a judiciary—standard laws and a legal structure to rule on them, instead of arbitrary rule by a privileged class. Then, one by one, the colonies were granted limited self-government on the legislative level.

The structure, based on the Constitutional Act of 1791, was a transition between the old colonial system and independence, and was modeled after the British government. The Executive Council—the Governor and Ministers who administered law—was appointed. The Legislative Council, which made the laws, was appointed. The Assembly was elected.

It was not really a viable form of government, for the Legislative Council, which was generally composed of "Anglican gentlemen," was in constant conflict with the Assembly, which was likely to be composed of merchants of all denominations. At first the Assembly was called for strictly "advisory" purposes. But gradually it became stronger, more important. By the mid-1800s, Great Britain was beginning to listen to the colonial assemblies rather than to fishing admirals and autocratic governors.

The struggle of the British North American colonies for representative government became a large-scale battle in Lower and Upper Canada, where a number of conflicts brewed. Upper Canada around the Great Lakes, which had been largely settled by small farmers and U.E. Loyalists from the United States, had a situation similar to the Maritimes'. A privileged class of Anglicans gained a stranglehold on the colonial government soon after the American Revolution. Other Protestants, Roman Catholics, and indeed most of the poorer Anglicans suffered discrimination or could not vote because of stiff property limitations. And as on PEI, the farmers who actually broke the land could not get clear titles to their farms. The assemblies they elected became increasingly radical.

In Lower Canada, the struggle for representative government apparently ran along ethnic lines. Basically, the French-speaking majority of *habitants* was dominated by a minority of *Anglais* merchants. In the colonial government, only a few token *Canadiens* were given patronage or positions. But ethnic background was only an apparent division; the real division was along lines of class. The French-speaking hierarchy of the Roman Catholic

Church, for instance, was dominated by refugees from the French Revolution, who hated any form of republicanism. They tended to collaborate with the English-speaking merchants. Likewise, reformers were not limited to French Canadians. Many of the radical leaders in Lower Canadian politics were English-speaking, including some of Irish descent.

While French Canadians tended to blame their problems on the *Anglais* merchants, the merchants had problems of their own. They saw themselves as cut off from the great interior Plains and forests—and therefore expansion—by Upper Canada. At the same time *Canadiens* were clamoring for self-determination, the *Anglais* were howling for union with Upper Canada.

Lines were drawn. Conservative Anglicans in Upper Canada united with the Roman Catholic hierarchy and the frightened *Anglais* merchants of Lower Canada. Agrarian reformers around the Great Lakes joined forces with the French-speaking radicals along the St. Lawrence. In 1837, armed revolutions shook the colonial system to its roots.

Like the Indian troubles of Canada as compared to the terrible battles of the United States, Canada's revolutions were mere skirmishes compared to the American Revolution. The rebellion in Upper Canada was led by William Lyon Mackenzie, a fiery wisp of a newspaper editor and longtime member of the colonial Assembly, who took on the privileged Anglicans with rash courage but little popular support. In Lower Canada, the rebellion was led by Louis Papineau. Also a longtime assemblyman, Papineau certainly had popular support. The *habitants* fought to the death for him, and few of his fellow assemblymen were not implicated in the uprising. Nevertheless, the battles in both Canadas were brief, the rebellions failed, and Mackenzie and Papineau fled to the United States.

Of course, the defeat was only a minor setback. Inevitably, Lower and Upper Canada would gain representative government. But more importantly, people of different areas, languages, religions, races, and land systems would find a common ground for their battle. Something was forming which was larger than a single colony or culture. That something was a nation.

Why should seven distinct colonies—widely separated in geography and economy—form a nation? What did a Nova Scotian sailor have in common with a Hudson's Bay trader on the Pacific Coast? Or a lumber merchant of New Brunswick with an industrialist in Toronto or a *habitant* in Quebec? Very little, actually. The regions united not because of internal similarities, but in a sense to preserve the differences between them.

Industrialization was beginning. And to prosper in the new Industrial Age, or even to survive, the diverse Canadian cultures found they had to unite. They had to unite or be absorbed and lost in events that were shaping the modern world.

FORMATION OF THE MOSAIC

EIGHT

The Rebellions of 1837 were only a dramatic symptom of the changes that would actually create Canada during the first half of the nineteenth century. The external effect of the American Revolution was to establish Canadian boundaries. New Brunswick, with its large Loyalist immigration, was carved out of Nova Scotia. And the southern boundary of the mainland was drawn roughly along the 49th parallel. The War of 1812, however, was more important to Canada's future nationhood than the American Revolution.

The War of 1812 was a fruitless war, dignified only by several dramatic sea battles. The only clear motive for it was the fate of the Canadian fur trade, and that was virtually unchanged by the fighting. New England was so disgruntled by the wanton hostilities that it insisted on staying out of the war and in carrying on commerce with the "enemy," Britain. Yet this war so impressed Canadians that they refer to it even today.

Canada was attacked by the United States. From the U.S. point of view, British North America was the last bitter bastion of English dominance on the continent. And surely, thought the patriots, the common people of Canada would rise en masse and joyfully welcome their liberators. The conquest of Canada was to be "a mere matter of marching." It wasn't.

The U.S. struck at Upper Canada, burning and pillaging the southernmost settlements around the Great Lakes. Sir Isaac Brock and the Indian nationalist Tecumseh launched a counterattack and took Detroit, which surrendered without a shot. Then in September 1813, Commodore Perry achieved a stunning victory on the crucial Great Lakes, opening the way to the invasion of Upper Canada, and in the Battle of the Thames in October, Tecumseh was killed. But the U.S. force, though large, was ill-trained and badly led, and it was soon pushed back by the Canadian settlers.

Likewise, in Lower Canada the United States staged invasions all along the St. Lawrence. But these were even less successful than in Upper Canada, and the native militia—consisting of French, English, and Indian alike—drove the invaders back. In the Maritimes, of course, the war took the form of individual piracy, in which neither side won.

In the end, when peace was declared in 1815, the territories remained just as they had been before the war. The only difference was that Canadians and *Canadiens* had decided, once and for all, that they were not a part of the United States.

The years that followed the War of 1812 have been called the Great Peace. It was a time when industry and commerce promised a good life for all, when both the United States and British North

America eagerly pressed forward with internal development, settling their differences in order to prosper. But during this so-called Great Peace, the greatest revolution ever known, the Industrial Revolution, was taking place. It shook the whole Western world to its very roots, and in its first shock, the lives of many people changed violently.

Many small farmers were displaced by mechanized farming equipment; they left the land for the dismal, filthy factory towns and mines. At the same time in the towns and cities, skilled artisans such as weavers, hosiers, lacemakers, and spinners were edged out by machines powered by steam. No longer protected by lord or guild, people were left to fend for themselves, look to their own interests, control their own destinies in this new world of competition and free enterprise. The Great Peace was really the Great Unrest, and it ended with the revolts that flared up all over Europe in 1848.

Revolution was one answer for displaced people; the other was to emigrate to North America. They came tightly packed in leaky, filthy ships where swift epidemics of cholera left many of their number dead. They arrived and filtered through Newfoundland and the Maritimes to new homes all over the country. Here they broke land for farms, lumbered the forests, and labored in the cities and on the canals.

Unlike England, Canada had little heavy industry. It was a colonial country of raw resources. Wheat, potash, and furs were exported in large quantities, but the up-and-coming resource was timber. After Napoleon cut off Britain's supply of wood from the Baltic in 1806, Canadian timber was unchallenged; it came to account for a third of the colonies' exports.

At first the logs were squared with a broad-axe and floated down the St. Lawrence and the rivers of New Brunswick in huge rafts. By midcentury, however, sawmills were coming into their own, and sawn lumber was filling the ships to England. Many of the towns, such as Saint John, New Brunswick, and Toronto, Ontario, were largely built on timber-making and lumbering, and many of the leading families made their wealth in the trade.

Because of British North America's role as a supplier of raw materials, the main effects of the Industrial Revolution on it was not in industry, but in transportation. In Canada, "transportation" meant "boat," and it was the day of the wooden ship. Shipbuilding in Quebec, New Brunswick, and especially Nova Scotia was in its heyday.

Well into the twentieth century, Nova Scotia had very few roads. Founded on fishing, all of the little towns lay on the coasts; the interior, with its deer paths and tiny trails, was more or less left to the Indians. All of the villages on the Atlantic and the Bras d'Or Lakes received their provisions from little boats engaged in this trade, rather than by land.

As the trade with New England and the West Indies flourished, shipbuilding became a major enterprise. At Sydney, Lunenburg, and Halifax, there were large companies run by wealthy families and employing numerous shipwrights and laborers. But many more ships were built by local coal or timber merchants and farmers in the little villages. By the 1850s, for instance, Baddeck on Cape Breton Island prospered to the point of obtaining its own Shipping Registry Office, thus putting it on equal footing with Sydney—though Baddeck was just a tiny village (and always would be), while Sydney was a small city.

Since there were more ships than needed for the local trade, timber and labor being so plentiful, it was common to sell a new ship at the end of its first or second voyage. It was even more common to load a ship with cargo for a certain destination, perhaps the West Indies or New England, and leave it to the captain to find another cargo destined for another port. Some of these voyages took two or three years and carried the crew halfway around the world.

In Central Canada, too, the main thrust of industrialization

was in transportation. The steamship took to the inland waterways and came into its own when the United States opened the
Erie Canal in 1825.

This drew shipping away from the St. Lawrence. Upper Canada in response began a series of St. Lawrence canals, beginning
with the Welland, opened in 1829. Then the United States discovered its vast West, and left off canal building for railroad building. It embarked on a great transcontinental railroad, which again
threatened and stimulated Canadian business interests.

Canada's first railroads were little "portage" lines, which
shuttled between the major waterways. Then an "inter-colonial"
railroad was built by some London investors at great expense to
the Canadian public. Called the Grand Trunk Railway, it began a
line between Quebec and Ontario in 1853, and eventually serviced
a number of U.S. towns south of the Great Lakes. Also in the
1850s, a powerful financier named Alexander Galt completed a
railroad between Montreal and Portland, Maine, which would at
last give St. Lawrence traffic an ice-free winter port.

By this time, the Canadian business interests had discovered
their own great West and were determined to build their own
transcontinental railroad. But to encourage industry, build great
railroads, and claim the West would require a larger power base
than local, or even regional, interests. It would require a "nation." The high-rolling, big-spending politics of railroad building,
land speculation, and commerce produced a group of politicians
whose base was inter-colonial, or "national."

On the national level all over the Western world, great political changes accompanied the Industrial Revolution. In Britain, the
conflict was between privilege, as represented by the landed gen-
try, and progress, as represented by the new industrialists. The
new breed in Parliament—the Liberals—believed that each colony, each market, each individual, must stand on its own. They
advocated free trade and free competition—a *laissez faire* economy. Buy at the cheapest market and sell at the dearest was the

ideal. They saw the old colonial system as hampering progress and industry.

In the United States, the conflict was not so much between privilege and progress as between East and West. The East Coast financial powers promoted a highly centralized government which would use the resources of other regions to build up industry. The small southern farmers and western pioneers, on the other hand, distrusted "big business" and "the East." They wanted local power, universal suffrage, and a bit of land for everyone. From them came the hue and cry of Manifest Destiny—the doctrine that claimed it was the United States' "manifest destiny" to spread over the whole continent so that every U.S. citizen might become a landowner, at least with some small farm or house. Manifest Destiny was a powerful principle and one which threatened both Mexico and Canada.

Canada, a colony of Britain yet geographically more akin to the United States, combined both these conflicts. In Upper Canada, for instance, the privileged class attached to the Anglican Church was pitted against the struggling frontier farmers. The farmers found little difficulty in allying themselves with the Liberals whose great industrial progress (and railroads) was held up by the rigid control of the privileged. This alliance would eventually result in Confederation or "nationhood."

Just as the thirteen U.S. colonies had waged their struggle for independence with the cry for "representative government," the rallying point for the establishment of the Canadian nation was "responsible government." Proponents of Confederation considered "responsible" government a further democratic evolution of "representative." Though unfamiliar in the United States, the idea of responsible government is common in European countries that have parliamentary systems. It means in essence that the government is "responsible" to the people it governs, rather than to the King or Queen or their representative, the Governor.

The British parliamentary system is bicameral, with an

elected House of Commons and an appointed or inherited House of Lords (Britain) or Senate (Canada). Most of the activity of the national government is focused into these two legislative bodies— though in Canada the appointed house, the Senate, is much less important than Britain's House of Lords. The House of Commons is directly "responsible" to the electorate, and the executive is responsible to the legislature.

The federal government of Canada, since 1867, is headed by the King or Queen of England, who is represented in Canada by the Governor General. This Governor General has no real power, and mainly functions at ceremonies. The real chief executive is the Prime Minister and the Cabinet, chosen by "responsible" process; that is, the political party that wins the most number of seats in the House of Commons takes over the executive. The leader of this party becomes the Prime Minister. If the Prime Minister is defeated on any major piece of legislation, a new election is called, whereas in the U.S., the President remains in office for a set term, even if the President's party is not in the majority in Congress and the legislation the President supports is defeated. Responsible government tends to tie all branches of government together, instead of setting them against one another. There are no "checks and balances" as in the United States system.

Canada was to adapt this British institution to American frontier democracy. The battle for responsible government in Canada was a battle for nationhood. In the Rebellions of 1837, the forces of self-determination (Lower Canada) and reform (Upper Canada) were pitted against colonialism and privilege.

The conservative reaction to the Rebellions was the Act of Union of 1841, which combined Upper and Lower Canada into one unit, and wiped out French as an official language. The Upper Canadian ruling class pushed for Union because Upper Canada was bankrupted by the canal building. Lower Canada, which refused to get involved in those enterprises, had a very low debt and sound finances.

The only group in Lower Canada that wanted Union, however, was the *Anglais* merchants. After the defeat of the North
West Company, they saw themselves confined to a narrow cell
within a French-speaking region. Their ability to expand was cut
off geographically from the great hinterland of the West by Upper
Canada. They pressed for Union: it would offset the terrifying
French majority that surrounded them, and give them access to the
lands of the West. The *Canadiens,* of course, saw the denial of
their language as an attack upon their very existence.

Union under the thumb of the Canadian Tories was as unrealistic as the Rebellions of 1837. It never worked. Its strains became critical when economic disaster hit Canada in 1846–47. The
timber boom turned into a bust, bankrupting lumber speculators,
closing down lumber camps and sawmills. At about the same
time, the British Whigs led Britain to adopt free trade, ending the
trade preferences which had been so profitable to Canada. At the
same time, the United States put severe restrictions on merchan-
dise being shipped from the United States to England via the St.
Lawrence—which had been another source of Canadian profits. In
New Brunswick and Central Canada, where lumbering or laboring
on the canals was the only way many extremely poor immigrants
had of making a living, the collapse of the timber industry and St.
Lawrence commerce brought terrible misery, sometimes starvation.

It took little to topple the old colonial system. French-speaking radicals allied with English-speaking reformers. In 1848, a
reform administration committed to "responsible government"
swept into office, marking the end of privilege and narrow interests. It marked the beginning of progress.

It had taken a decade to solve the conflict between privilege
and progress. It would take two decades more to resolve the
conflict between East and West—that is, between the cities of Ontario and Quebec, and the frontier of Ontario and the Plains. In
western Ontario, frontier democracy had taken hold among the

small farmers, but the Canadian variation was much more radical, vocal, and firmly entrenched than in the United States. Focused into the Clear Grits Party and led by the implacable newspaper editor George Brown, the farmers denounced "Big Business in the East" and called for "Rep by Pop," or representation by population rather than by area.

Unlike the United States, Central Canada not only had a West; it also had an East—the Maritimes. Maritimers were more connected to England and New England than to Canada and stood to gain nothing from Confederation. In Lower Canada, the Québécois feared, with a good deal of justification, any union which might further submerge their culture.

The majority of people in all the regions did not particularly want Confederation. It took two great factors to transcend this resistance. The first was the determination of a group of powerful "inter-colonial" financiers and politicians to build a railroad. The second was the threat posed from the south by the United States.

We can best judge what group in Canadian society stood to gain the most from Confederation by looking at the men involved. The idea itself was a financial scheme of Alexander Galt, land speculator, railroad builder, financier. The Maritimes were brought in by Charles Tupper, who later became Minister of Railroads. Quebec was brought in by George Cartier, an anglicized French Canadian, lawyer for the Grand Trunk Railway. They had in mind a highly centralized government, a "nation," which would control the rest of the country for the greater good of industry and speculative finance.

But in the final result, this powerful impulse was modified and broadened by the profound regional pressures. Confederation had to satisfy the suspicions of the West, the fears of the Québécois, the livelihood of the Maritimers. Confederation had to take all these things into consideration. It was quite a strain.

In the two decades between self-government and Confederation, principal leaders fought and maneuvered for supremacy over one another. Given a weak national government, they pulled this way and that, sometimes managing to bring down the ministry of their foes, sometimes combining with their foes to oppose yet another faction. By the 1860s, however, several individuals who could transcend the narrow interests, both commercial and regional, emerged from the conflict.

D'Arcy McGee was the "voice" of Confederation. In the United States a group of Irish-Americans called Fenians, who hated England, were determined with rash courage to drive the British from the continent, annexing Canada to the United States. D'Arcy McGee was an ex-Fenian, who translated Irish nationalism into Canadian nationalism. He was a spellbinding speaker and traveled all over Canada putting forth the idea of Confederation.

But the Father of Confederation was John A. Macdonald, a brilliant politician of Highland Scots descent. Macdonald was involved in railroad politics and so had a vested interest in Confederation. But his real love was politics itself, and building a "nation" was more important to him than the narrow world of finances. His gift was for practical politics, for reconciling seemingly unreconcilable differences, and acquiring compromise from uncompromising factions. The worst of him was that he was an opportunist, never one to hold to an ideal when expediency was involved.

The best of Macdonald is epitomized by his attitude toward the French Canadians. "If a Lower Canadian Britisher desires to conquer," he said, ". . . he must make friends with the French . . . he must respect their nationality. Treat them as a nation, and they will act as free people generally do—generously. Treat them as a faction and they become factious." He convinced *Canadien* leaders that their culture would be preserved. He convinced the Maritime politicians that Confederation would be more financially beneficial than free trade independence. He convinced George Brown that a railroad meant land for small farmers in the West.

Still there might not have been Confederation without a stimulus from the United States. First there was the financial competition. In the early 1800s, for instance, U.S. financier John Jacob Astor had tried to take over Canada's fur trade from the Nor'Westers. Likewise, Nova Scotia jealously guarded its fisheries from New Englanders, and New Brunswick lumber barons fought with Maine over the precious forests. On the Plains, U.S. whisky traders had invaded and established forts right under the nose of the Hudson's Bay Company.

More disturbing than even the economic threat was the physical one. Tacitly encouraged by the United States, Fenians staged attacks all along the border, burning churches and farms as they went. Added to this was the prospect of hordes of Union soldiers returning north from the Civil War. The need for unity among the British North American colonies became critical.

In the end, Newfoundland did not join in Confederation, and tiny Prince Edward Island held out for equal representation with the larger regions. But Nova Scotia, New Brunswick, Ontario (Upper Canada, then Canada West), and Quebec (Lower Canada, then Canada East) united as the Dominion of Canada on July 1, 1867.

Between Montreal and Toronto, a new capital was established, named Ottawa. The name "Canada," an Iroquoian word meaning "village," first used for the area by the explorer Jacques Cartier, was applied to the whole country. The term "Dominion" was adopted, rather than "republic" or "kingdom," from Psalm 72: "He shall have dominion also from sea to sea, and from the river unto the ends of the earth."

Even today, Canada's impulse toward unification is offset by the strong individual regions. Isolated from one another by the rugged terrain, each with its own long history and distinct economy, the provinces retained their own characters to a degree which the states did not. And while the United States calls itself a "melting pot," Canadians call their country a "mosaic."

Fishing and lumbering are two of Canada's principal industries. Above: In New-foundland, split and salted cod are spread to cure in the sun. (*Canadian Government Travel Bureau*) Right: A pulp and paper mill in Trois Rivières, Quebec. (*Canadian Department of External Affairs*)

A painting by Robert Hariss shows John Macdonald (standing, c.) and the Canadian leaders who brought about Confederation in 1867. (*Public Archives of Canada*)

Beyond this church in Nova Scotia lies the land from which the Acadians were expelled by the English in 1755. (*Canadian Government Travel Bureau*)

Parliament buildings overlook the St. Lawrence in Canada's capital, Ottawa. (*Canadian Department of External Affairs*)

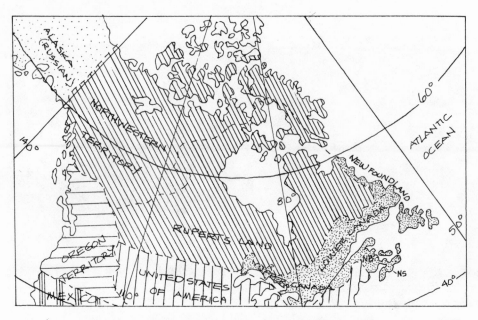

The international boundary was extended along the 49th parallel in 1818. By 1825 Great Britain and Russia had agreed on the boundary of Alaska.

In 1867 the Dominion of Canada was established.

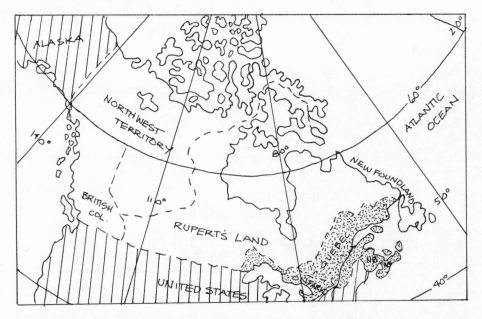

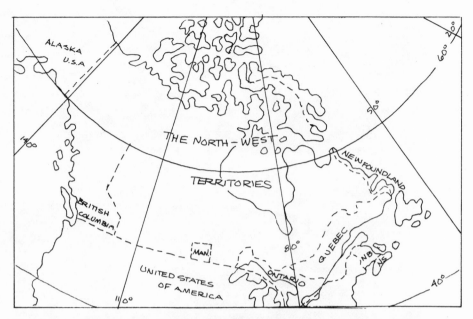

British Columbia joined the Dominion in 1871 and Prince Edward Island in 1873. Meanwhile Canada had acquired the Northwest Territories from the Hudson's Bay Company and Manitoba had been created as a province.

In 1949 Newfoundland joined the Confederation, the tenth and last province. (*Beth McBride*)

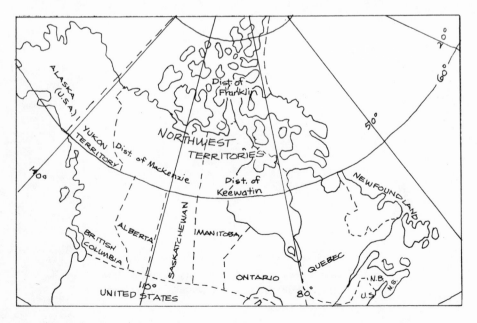

Orchards deep in Canada's "Valley of the Sun," the Okanagan Valley in British Columbia. (*Canadian Government Travel Bureau*)

Vast farmlands in Saskatchewan stretch as far as the eye can see. (*Canadian Department of External Affairs*)

The *Labrador* works her way through the ice of the Gulf of the St. Lawrence, Quebec. (*Canadian Department of External Affairs*)

The Royal Canadian Mounted Policemen perform their traditional "Musical Ride." (*Canadian Government Travel Bureau*)

John A. Macdonald became Prime Minister after
Confederation, and he dominated federal politics
for Canada's first generation, until his death in
1891. He formed his Cabinet from representatives
of diverse regions and special interests, accommo-
dating most of the opposing forces in Canada to
"national" ends.

Those ends were formulated in Macdonald's
so-called National Policy, which boiled down to
three major goals: the abolishment of free trade and
the enactment of high tariffs on foreign manufactures; the building of a transcontinental railroad;
and the settlement of the West.

The first goal represented the interest of the industrial and commercial complex which was developing in Toronto and Montreal. Canada's own fledgling industries would never get breathing space to develop if they had to compete with cheaper goods from other countries, and industrial leaders demanded some "protection" in the form of tariffs. The second two points of the National Policy—the acquisition of the wilderness to the west and the transcontinental railroad—reflected the need of the industrial complex for a vast hinterland to supply the eastern cities.

The Dominion government was intended to be highly centralized. It is both parliamentary like Britain's, and federal like the United States'. There are two levels of government, federal and provincial, and of these the federal level was to be the more important. The Fathers of Confederation saw the provinces as remaining colonies—but colonies of Central Canada instead of Britain.

Each province was left with much the same government it had developed as a colony. Quebec was guaranteed its own language, religion, and *Canadien* civil code by the British North American (BNA) Act, which serves Canada as a constitution. The provinces were given jurisdiction over what seemed at the time to be minor, local concerns: education, property and civil rights, social welfare, housing, municipal institutions, and resources within provincial boundaries.

The federal government was given all the major powers— taxation, banking, defense, trade and commerce, shipping, fisheries—and all powers not assigned to the provincial governments resided with the federal government. All this, of course, was designed to place control in the hands of the federal government, so that the whole vast country would become centered on Montreal-Toronto-Ottawa, where resided commerce, industry, and federal government.

Centralization did not work out as the Confederalists planned. To a much greater extent than in the United States, the regions of Canada were separated from one another both geographically and historically. Each had its own distinct character. Under a faraway France or England, they had even developed their own social structure, institutions, and colonial governments. By the end of the nineteenth century the BNA Act was being given a different interpretation. A British court, the Judicial Committee of the Privy Council, broadened the powers of the provinces, putting vast new areas under their control.

Immediately after Confederation in 1867, the public said its piece in the general elections. The pro-Confederation governments in New Brunswick and Nova Scotia were ousted, and even the popular George Brown of the Clear Grits lost in Ontario. The most general resentment was toward Macdonald's tariffs. Tariffs protect industry from foreign competition. But they are eventually paid for by the consumers, who pay higher prices for their everyday goods. Most Canadians, especially in the Maritimes, wanted no tariffs. They wanted free trade. Free trade was a Liberal platform, while industry's representatives in government were Conservatives. John A. Macdonald was a Conservative.

In addition, each former colony lost control of its natural resources—the potentially great West in the case of Ontario, and the fisheries and shipping trade in the Maritimes. Nova Scotians insisted they had been "sold at 84 cents a head," or that their independent rights had been bargained away to the cause of Confederation, and they sent a representative to London to discuss secession.

Likewise, for Canada to claim and secure British Columbia, the colony on its other coast, was a strain. British Columbia was a world apart, separated from the rest of Canada by the impassable Shield muskeg of western Ontario, the vast wilderness of the central Plains, and a series of mountain ranges, terrain unknown. How this province came to belong to Canada rather than the United States is more history than geography.

The British colony on the Pacific Coast centered in Victoria on Vancouver Island, until the first gold rush of the 1850s. In addition to 3,000 Indians, the island contained 1,000 white settlers, 600 of them children, and all of them employees or family with the Hudson's Bay Company. They were, it is said, more British than the British. When gold was found on the Fraser River, 10,000 prospectors rushed in, many of them from California, overwhelming the adult colonists more than 20 to 1.

Victoria at this time was blessed with a broad-minded, level-headed, thoroughly just Governor, James Douglas, who was also the Hudson's Bay Company's Chief Factor, or chief administrator, west of the mountains. He declared the mainland to be Crown Lands, enabling him to impose some order. So rigid and fair was his sense of justice, and so swiftly did he capture any wrongdoer, that British Columbia escaped the rough history of the California gold camps. In Canada, miners found they did not have to wear guns.

But barely had Douglas pacified the mainland than Canada suffered another trauma. Gold was found in extravagant quantities far north of settlement, in the region of Cariboo Lake. Thousands of people streamed in to tackle the closely packed mountains of the north, with peaks of 6,000 feet, rugged gorges, and thick forests. There was only an occasional Indian path or bridge to guide them. Douglas met this crisis with a remarkable feat: the building of the Cariboo Road to the gold country. Knowing that the great distance would require large supply trains, he insisted that the road be at least 18 feet wide for all of its 400-mile length.

Then the boom which enriched Victoria and established the mainland vanished as quickly as it had come. In its wake came a collapse of economic activity. Merchants waited in vain for the boatloads of prospectors. Out-of-work miners, stranded and desperate by the end of the strike, filed aimlessly through the now-dreary boom towns.

The immigrants from the United States began agitating for annexation to the U.S. as a solution to economic woes. The Britishers of course shrank in horror at such disloyalty to the Crown.

Numerically weak but politically strong, they began a campaign of their own. At its head was an extraordinary reformist politician named William Smith. Because such a common name was often confused by the post office, he changed it to Amor de Cosmos— "Lover of the Universe." Flamboyant, eloquent, and multilingual, he lived up to the name, and dominated politics in British Columbia for many years. At this early stage he was pro-Confederation, and he stilled the voices for annexation to the United States, eventually leading the colony into the Dominion.

The Macdonald administration somehow managed to hold the territory from sea to sea, standing in the middle of a continent with a straining province on either hand. Nova Scotia was quieted down with the guarantee of additional subsidies. British Columbia was wooed and won in 1871, with the promise of the railroad across the continent. Little Prince Edward Island, plagued with debts and its settlers unable to clear title to their lands from absentee landlords, succumbed to Confederation in 1873.

But having the two coasts was not enough; Canada also had to have its vast interior, the Plains, then called Rupert's Land.

At the time of Confederation, there were at most 40,000 people on the Plains. The majority, 25,000, were Indians—Cree, Sioux, Assiniboine, and on the far Plains, the three tribes (Blackfoot, Blood, and Piegan), that had joined together as the Blackfoot nation. Most settlers with fields and permanent houses lived along the banks of the Red River. Most were half-breeds, or Métis. There were 6,000 French-speaking and 4,000 English-speaking Métis (descendants of French or Scots traders and Cree), and 1,500 Anglos. Isolated from eastern Canada by the Shield, the Red River settlement developed a remarkable society.

Plains culture was at its peak. Acquiring horses enabled the Indians to build tall, elegant tepees, for horses were able to drag longer *travois,* with longer lodge poles, than their predecessors, dogs. And now with the gun, hunters could provide plenty of skins to cover the poles. The buffalo hunt was at its height, with dramatic exhibitions of skill, as horse and rider plunged into the midst of the herds, riding alongside the gigantic beasts to get a close shot. Such drama required appropriate ceremonies, and the early dances for rain or luck in finding herds became elaborate, many-colored rituals.

In addition to the Indians who held territory in Canada, there were those who had migrated from the United States. When the Union Pacific and Central Pacific built the transcontinental railroad across the United States, it divided the overall buffalo population into two parts, because the buffalo would not cross the tracks. The southern herd in the United States was quickly wiped out, for there hunters killed the beasts by the thousands, just for their tongues and hides. The carcasses were left to rot. The northern herd survived a little longer, and so the Indians who lived by buffalo followed it north.

But the tracks were only part of it. The United States was intent on driving the Indians off the continent or, that failing, killing them. The really desperate wars began when the U.S. army tried to remove Indians from fertile land to make room for white settlers, forcing the natives onto barren reservations. The Indians resisted, usually won the first skirmishes, then were overwhelmed by the massive armies sent against them. Band after band with its children, elderly people, and wounded, made a desperate dash northward. For the Indians had always found friendship among the Red Riverites, and by the time of Confederation had discovered the value of the "medicine line," the border between the United States and Canada. North of that line was the "land where treaties are not broken," where lived the kindred Métis, and where the U.S. army could not follow.

Less settled than their *Canadien* forebears, but more settled than the Indian bands, the Métis' life-style included farming, trading, and in the summer, the buffalo hunt. Most Métis had strip farms in the French tradition along the banks of the Red River, where they cultivated vegetables and grains. They trapped fur-bearing animals in the winter, and left the farm—sometimes taking the whole family—to join the Indians in the great buffalo hunts of spring and summer.

The buffalo hides they collected were carted south to St. Paul, Minnesota, which was the natural center for the Métis. The most common form of transportation was the remarkable Red River cart. The cart was square with high rails and was drawn by one animal, usually an ox. It was light enough to negotiate the sticky Plains mud that followed the rains and strong enough to carry a ton of goods. The two wheels, which were five or six feet high, could be easily removed at rivers, so that the cart became a raft. And it could be repaired very easily, with all wood parts or, Métis claimed, the jawbone of a moose. Because grease for lubrication mixed with the Plains dust and wore down the wheels, no lubrication was used. The disadvantage to this convenience was a hellish noise that could be heard for miles across the Plains. In later years, when the buffalo had disappeared from the Plains, the Indians used to tease their Métis friends, saying that the beasts had fled to escape the noise of the carts.

Métis society developed a good deal beyond the level of bare living. Under the lax administration of the Hudson's Bay Company, many Métis became respectable citizens, and the largest houses in settlement towns belonged to them. They often sent their most promising youngsters to Montreal to be educated, and they carried on as much government as was needed.

With the Confederation came the first land sharks, the fringe element of big business in the East. They professed to be patriots and called themselves Canada Firsters, meaning they wanted the West *annexed* to Canada as a territory or colony of Ontario, rather than *federated* as a province of Canada. And they were the same ones who sought to suppress Québécois culture back in Central Canada. The Métis? Why, they were just more lazy, backward

French, and worse, mongrel half-breeds. And the Indians? Savages.

One such Canadian Firster was Charles Mair, who was attached to an annexationist newspaper in Toronto. Shortly after arriving in Winnipeg, he wrote a series of letters which were reprinted in the Toronto *Globe*. Of course, Mair never dreamed that these "backward" Plains people ever read newspapers from Toronto. "Many wealthy people here," he wrote, "are married to half-breed women, who, having no coat of arms but a 'totem' to look back to, make up for this deficiency by biting at the backs of their 'white' sisters." He soon got his answer, and at the hands of one of the "white" sisters. The next time he walked into the general store, Mrs. A. G. B. Bannatyne, who owned it, who was a leading citizen, and who was *not* a Métis, seized a horsewhip from the wall and whipped him halfway down the street.

It was in this atmosphere that, overnight, the Canadian government and the Hudson's Bay Company agreed to transfer the Plains territory from the Company to Canada. The federal government did not consult with the settlers; it did not even notify them. They found out from the newspapers.

What this meant to the Red Riverites on a practical level was that their whole livelihood was threatened. The buffalo would be driven away by extensive settlement. Their trade with St. Paul would become illegal. And worst of all, their land, which was farmed the Quebec way, in strip farms along the river, would be slashed by the square townships that the Canadian government intended to impose. To add insult to injury, the new Governor was the editor of Mair's newspaper from Toronto. In 1870, the furious Métis met to decide their next step.

As Douglas Hill points out in *The Opening of the Canadian West,* what followed was not a "rebellion" but a quite legal "resistance." The Red Riverites mainly wanted to negotiate. They chose as their leader a twenty-four-year-old Métis named Louis Riel, who had been educated in Montreal. The ranks were filled by rough buffalo hunters, who imposed on themselves the discipline of the buffalo hunt. They even swore off alcohol for the duration of the resistance.

Most of the Red Riverites, including the English-speaking Métis, fell in behind this group. Hudson's Bay agents openly sympathized, and the Catholic Church supported it wholeheartedly. A few priests even joined the ranks. The resisters turned back the Governor, and took over the Hudson's Bay's Fort Garry without a fight. And when the Governor led the sixty-odd Canada Firsters against them, they took the Firsters captive without a shot.

The Macdonald government calmed the resistance by promising that all Métis property rights and religious liberties would be preserved, and by accepting a delegation of prominent Métis in Ottawa. The delegation returned from Ottawa with the concession of 1,400,000 acres reserved for the Métis, with safeguards for the French language and Catholic religion, and with provincial (rather than territorial) status for the Red River area, now renamed Manitoba, which was created in 1870.

Within a few years, the only one of these concessions that remained secure was the provincial status. Riel himself went into exile in the U.S. The land reserved for the Métis quickly disappeared. When a band of Métis left their land for their seasonal buffalo hunting, they often came back to find new settlers had moved in. Having no recourse in the face of the hostile soldiers who policed them, many of the disgusted Métis simply moved west, out onto the Plains where no settlers had yet arrived. Barely a decade later, they would have to make another stand.

In the meantime violence, stimulated mainly by whisky traders from the United States and their companions, the "wolfers," was breaking out all over the Plains. The wolfers killed wolves and coyotes for their skins by poisoning the carcasses of buffalo. This infuriated the Indians, whose leaders hinted that if the Canadian government did not get rid of the wolfers and whisky traders, their people would. When a group of wolfers and whisky traders from Fort Benton, Montana, massacred a band of Indians in the Cypress Hills of Canada, Ottawa feared there would be a general Indian uprising.

Macdonald immediately presented a bill to Parliament which created the North-West Mounted Police, consisting of three hundred highly trained and educated men. The Mounties were not an army but a police unit, and so came under civilian control. They brought order, not with violence, but with authority.

Their first job was to get rid of the whisky traders. With a huge wagon train that stretched out for four miles, the Mounties struggled through the muskeg of the Shield and the dust of the Plains. The oxen and horses began to die, and at some points the men actually carried the horses, for miles. It took them eighty-eight days to cross the Plains and reach the infamous center of whisky trading, Fort Whoop-Up, near the U.S. border. When they arrived, they found that all the traders had fled leaving only a U.S. flag behind.

This set the general tone of the Mounties' administration. They seldom resorted to force, relying instead on their authority with frontier folk, and on their reputation for fair play and courage among the Indians. At each post they took over, they usually had only to ''show the flag'' to establish order.

The most important undertaking of the Mounties was to negotiate treaties with the Plains Indians. Communities of Sioux were now pouring into Canada to escape U.S. reprisals after the Battle of the Little Big Horn. The great Sitting Bull himself arrived in 1877. The government set about quietly establishing small reservations.

Meanwhile, U.S. troops stationed just south of the border chafed at the knowledge that the Sioux were safe on the other side. Then they found a long-range solution to their problem. The soldiers started a series of prairie fires along the border, wildfires that cut wide swathes through the dry prairie grasses. Now even the northern herd was trapped inside the United States, where the slaughter continued with rapid efficiency. By 1877, the buffalo were nearly extinct, and the Canadian Indians, their numbers swelled by the Plains immigrants, competed for the few that remained.

It was primarily the Mounties, the Hudson's Bay Company, and the missionaries who calmed the troubled waters and offered the Indians an alternative to war and starvation. The great leaders such as Crowfoot and Sitting Bull knew their way of life was over and decided to get the best possible deal for their people in a changing world. Equally great chiefs, such as Big Bear of the Cree, refused to surrender their ancestral lands. Yet even their resistance was passive; they just wanted to be left alone. And for a time, until 1884, there was peace.

Macdonald remained uncharacteristically ignorant of the Métis and the Indians, ignorant of actual living conditions in his great West, because he was involved in messy railroad financing. The Canadian government had promised, when British Columbia agreed to join the Confederacy in 1871, that a railroad linking the Pacific and Atlantic coasts would be built. Macdonald, in fact, cheerfully offered to begin it within two years and complete it within ten. But by 1880 the British Columbians could see no trace of the railroad making its way across the Plains.

What held it up was the cost and the politics. For one thing, Macdonald demanded an all-Canadian route, with no dips south into the United States, and Canadian terrain was much more rugged than the United States. For another thing, Macdonald needed all-Canadian financing, which was a more difficult problem than even the terrain. Canadian capital was still undeveloped and would be strained to carry the burden of such a project by itself, without international investors from England or the United States.

Macdonald was caught up in a chaotic swirl of high finance and international deals. In the bitter political campaign Macdonald waged in 1872, prominent members of government accepted large campaign contributions from Canada Pacific Railway (CPR), which then received the contract for the proposed railroad to British Columbia. When this Pacific Scandal broke out, Macdonald was forced to resign. In the five years he was out of power, little was done to build the railroad.

Then in 1877, Macdonald came back into office, ready to roll, and brought in William Van Horne, perhaps the best railroad manager in the world. An engineering genius and a powerful administrator, he could play poker and drink all night and work through the next day and night without stopping. He half drove, half inspired his builders to do the impossible. He was, in short, a match for Canada's land. He conquered the Canadian terrain in three years, from 1882 to 1885, a feat considered the most dazzling of its time.

The Shield country north of Lake Superior presented the greatest challenge. One stretch of muskeg swallowed up the track seven times, three of those times taking a locomotive too. On the Plains, Van Horne drove his workers to break all records, laying 400 miles of track in one short summer. In mountainous British Columbia, no rock cutting equipment could be brought up the steep slopes, so the road was carved out of the granite by hand. Much of the mountain labor was done by several thousand Chinese. They had one of the roughest sections of the whole line. Spurs of solid granite rose hundreds of feet above deep gorges and canyons, requiring workers to be as adept at mountain climbing as at building.

With breathtaking daring and terrifying speed, Van Horne rushed the railroad across the continent, and by 1884, the end was in sight. Then the money ran out. Macdonald had pushed Parliament far enough and was besieged by critics. Just when support was needed most, Macdonald met blank walls on all sides. Then the West again erupted into war, and this saved the day.

The second Riel Rebellion was more serious, more deadly, than the first. The Plains Indians were in a particularly desperate state. Smallpox had swept through the tribes like prairie fire, and whole bands were wiped out by the epidemic. Further, the buffalo became almost extinct in the 1870s, so that by 1880, nearly all the Indians had lost their livelihood. Now for the most part limited to reserves, they were dependent on the Canadian government. But the government, having its own problems and never having been much aware of the Indians, ignored their plight and refused to send the provisions promised by treaties.

The Métis were also in a tough spot. Forced by white settlement and persecution out into the Plains, they had re-established themselves in the valley of the Saskatchewan River, and had broken the land, once again, into strip farms. And once again the surveyors followed.

As for the white settlers who farmed alongside the Métis, they too feared the encroaching government. They were trying to cope with the frontier agricultural problems of droughts and grasshopper plagues. Even at best the wheat was poor because of the short growing season. To expect them to comply with the strict homesteading regulations on top of this was too much to ask. The whites joined forces with the Métis, and at a general meeting the two peoples decided to ask Riel to return from exile to lead them.

Eventually a force of 8,000 Canadian soldiers was mustered against what surely could not have been more than 1,000 Indians, Métis, and white settlers. The rebels were more skillful and defeated the first armies sent against them. But finally they were crushed by the sheer weight of superior numbers and heavy artillery.

The principal leaders were tried in Regina. The trials became political rather than legal issues, which united the Québécois in a tremendous show of support for their French-speaking cousins. But Ontario wanted blood. The excuse was the execution of a Firster, Thomas Scott, during the first resistance in 1869. Riel probably could have claimed insanity and saved himself, but pleading insanity would have been akin to saying that everything his people had fought for was worth nothing. On November 16, 1885, Louis Riel was hanged.

The Rebellion had two profound effects on the "nation" of Canada. The first was that it alienated the Québécois (as *Canadiens* in Quebec now called themselves), not to mention the Métis, from the government that hanged Riel.

The second was that the railroad was saved. Through the snow and ice of a Canadian April, Van Horne rushed the soldiers over half-completed tracks. At each uncompleted section, he made sure there was hot food waiting, and sleighs to dash with soldiers over the snow to the next section of completed track. Van Horne got the first 5,000 troops to Winnipeg within ten days of the opening battle. Suddenly the railroad promoters were offered financing from all sides. And the railroad was completed on November 7, 1885, nine days before Louis Riel was hanged. With that, the West was won—or lost, depending on one's point of view.

A NATION WITH A DESTINY

But perhaps the real winning of the West came later. Perhaps the West was won less by the high-rolling railroad people than by the humble folk who actually settled the land. Settlers did not flock in the wake of the railroad, as the eastern business people and politicians had planned. They went instead to the United States where conditions of life and pioneering were easier. Canada was hard. In Canada one could spend a lifetime just trying to make one tiny scratch on those vast open Plains. It was a back-breaking, and often heart-breaking, job.

Grasshopper plagues destroyed crops; early frosts caught the still-ripening wheat in the fields;

severe droughts burned a whole year's labor to nothing. And worst of all was the terrible loneliness, people separated from each other by endless miles of Plains, and in the fierce winters completely cut off.

Where wood was not available to build houses, settlers used the one readily available resource: dirt. They dug into the sides of hills and lived like gophers, or cut "bricks" from sod to make the walls. In these "dug-outs" and "soddies," they lived in worse than primitive conditions. The women cleared land between trying to keep their families alive, and the young people, many still really children, hired themselves out as domestic help in the towns and sent their earnings home. The men sought odd jobs on the railroads until a farm could be started. Often too poor to afford draft animals, the settlers pulled plows themselves and walked great distances to find work. One Ukrainian walked 240 miles (in four days!) along the CPR tracks looking for work. This was what it took to conquer the West.

Canada ended up with a "mosaic" of cultures on its Plains because of railroad politics. To encourage railroad investors, the government had granted them huge tracts of land. The railroad promoters expected big profits from land sales. But nothing happened. So the Canadian government set about finding immigrants for the land promoters. Its most successful ventures involved large ethnic communities with strong traditional cultures. These often wanted to leave the Old World because of religious or cultural persecution.

A couple of early groups followed the creation of Manitoba in 1870. One of these, the Icelanders, founded a fishing and farming community named Gimli on the shores of Lake Winnipeg. But the most important group was the Mennonites. Originally driven from the Netherlands for refusing to bear arms, they had been a century in the Russian Ukraine when, once again, they were forced to emigrate.

They were used to the open steppes of the Ukraine, and

unlike the previous Plains settlers who had always settled around the rivers and lakes, the Mennonites moved out on the open prairie and broke the soil. With them they brought knowledge of crop rotation and summer fallowing, and a communal society. Each family owned its own farmhouse and garden, but the farmland was held in common. The sharing cut the costs of tools and seed greatly, and organized the farm labor efficiently. This system, their sound knowledge of Plains-type farming, and their daring in being first to wrestle with the open Plains combined to establish the Mennonites firmly. By 1876, they owned half a million acres of the richest prairie farmland in Manitoba.

Two decades passed after these original groups came before additional pioneers flooded in. Then in 1896, over ten years after Riel's death and the completion of the Canadian Pacific, the Liberals came into power. The Minister of the Interior, Clifford Sifton, came from Manitoba. The best examples of successful settlers Sifton knew were the Mennonites and Icelanders of his native Manitoba. The Plains, he thought, needed "stalwart peasants," tenth-generation farmers from the Old World. He made the terms of land ownership attractive and sent agents all over Europe.

Swedes and Finns, used to the woods of their homelands, began to establish themselves along the fringes of the Boreal Forest. Jews, fleeing the increasingly savage European pogroms, flooded into Winnipeg on the Red River, bringing with them few worldly goods, but considerable cultivation, education, and professionalism. Mormons came from the United States, where they were persecuted for their tradition of polygamy. They settled a million acres in Alberta and introduced irrigation. Hungarians were coaxed from the United States by enterprising Hungarian nobleman, Count Paul d'Esterhazy, who hired out as a colonizing agent for the Canadian Pacific. Ukrainians were led to the Plains by the great Ukrainian scientist Josef Oleskow. The first solid stream became a flood of many different peoples—Poles, Galicians, Czechs, Slovaks, Croats, Serbs—filling the Plains with many distinct cultures.

The Canadian government has crossed swords with only one of these groups, the Doukhobors from Russia. Like the Mennonites, the Dukhobors were pacifists and believed in the communal ownership of property. But they put more emphasis on mysticism than did the Mennonites and defended their culture fiercely. On several occasions the Canadian government pressed a Doukhobor sect on taxes, elementary education, or mystical practice. Always touchy about such interference with their "religious freedom," they were quick in protesting. Their protests took the form of a series of nude marches through the streets, which embarrassed the government into backing off. That, too, was the stuff of which pioneer immigrants were made.

The Canadian government never had cause to regret its encouragement of immigration. By 1905, less than a decade after Canada began this policy, the "third people" had been so successful in winning the Plains that Saskatchewan and Alberta were established as provinces and admitted to the Confederation.

The Chinese immigration to British Columbia, however, was less than welcome. The Pacific Coast whites were rabidly bigoted against the Orientals and worried ceaselessly about being overwhelmed by "the Yellow Peril." The British Columbian government tried to stop the immigration by passing laws. Time and again the Canadian government, which has the right to "disallow" provincial legislation, prevented those laws. Then with the completion of the railroad in 1885, the federal government itself no longer needed Chinese labor, and it let British Columbia impose a tax on Chinese immigrants.

Ironically, the Chinese immigration was hardly worth the uproar. While white British Columbia fretted about the Chinese during the late 1890s, it was being swamped by another immigration so huge as to make the Chinese immigration seem like a mere drop in the bucket. Gold had been discovered in the Klondike.

This was not the gold of the Cariboo which yielded a substantial profit of 10¢ per shovelful. This was gold that was worth an incredible $4 per shovelful, and it drove a whole continent mad.

Most of the gold-seekers did not know what they were getting into. They did not know the Canadian winter, nor the mountains in British Columbia, nor the hardships of the Yukon. Prospectors arrived at the base of Chilkoot Pass and camped for weeks, waiting in a single-file line of gold-seekers who marched over the icy pass for two full years.

Between White Horse and Dawson, there were, as the crow flies, nearly 300 miles of murderous mountain terrain. Many of the gold-seekers died; the survivors pushed on until they dropped from exhaustion. Some made it to Dawson, arriving in rags, with frost-bitten limbs, for the terrible winter of 1897. There was plently of gold. But all the gold in the world could not buy a plate of beans in Dawson that winter. Many of the folk who had made it through the mountains died of starvation.

The gold was soon gone. But during the course of the strike, British Columbia grew tremendously. And two new regions—the Yukon and the Peace River Valley of Alberta—were "discovered" by Canada. The Yukon was made a territory in 1896, with the capital at Dawson.

The "nation" as envisioned by Macdonald was now staked out. By early in the twentieth century, there were nine provinces instead of four, and the Plains had been settled. The regional strains on this "nation" were considerable. Yet there were vague stirrings of a real national spirit.

Nationalism was nurtured by a severe worldwide depression which lasted from 1873 to 1896, during which time the regions came to know their particular weaknesses and vulnerabilities. Obviously, British Columbia's greatest problem was its boom-and-bust economy. What British Columbians thought was their problem then—their proximity to the Orient—turned out to be one of their greatest assets. And on the Plains at this time, of course, the dry land problems of farmers, Indians, and Métis were at their worst, culminating in the rebellion during the 1880s.

In Ontario and Quebec, the small farms which had grown grain were no longer profitable because of competition from the Plains and the United States. Adjustment to a new agricultural economy would require a conversion to dairy, poultry, or fruit farming. But many of these farmers, grain growers for generations, knew nothing of these other kinds of farming; many did not have enough hard cash to make such a transition.

The Maritimes were particularly hard-hit. Now the great pine forests of New Brunswick were depleted, and the day of the wooden ship was over for Nova Scotia. There were still the fisheries and the coal in Nova Scotia, but these industries were dependent on the now-depressed economy of New England. Nor could trade sustain the people, for ocean-going ships sought other ports, up the St. Lawrence in the summer and through the United States in winter.

Newfoundland, with its marginal fishing economy, was the hardest hit of all. Since 1855, Newfoundland had been on its own, a self-governing community. The large fishing population had only seasonal employment, and this burden of a generally poor population was added to the debts Newfoundland ran up in trying to improve its harbor and build a railroad across the island. With the depression, the only remaining province-to-be floundered, and turned for help—not to England—but to Canada. It applied to Canada to be admitted to Confederation in 1895.

The great mover of Confederation, John A. Macdonald, had died several years before. Canada was not interested in one more burden after trying to cope with two decades of depression. Newfoundland then turned to England and was rebuffed. Finally the tough-spirited Prime Minister of Newfoundland, Robert Bond, secured a small loan on his own personal resources, which pulled Newfoundland through until the depression lifted. The people of Newfoundland paid for this enforced independence with ever-deepening poverty.

The economic woes were, of course, translated into political complaints. Ontario farmers blamed the cities for milking them, just as the Québécois blamed the *Anglais* for suppressing them. The Plains blamed their troubles on the monopoly that the federal government gave to the Canadian Pacific. The Maritimes blamed the government tariffs for their inability to compete. And Newfoundland, of course, never forgave Canada for deserting it in its most critical hour. For the next generation, any Newfie who so much as spoke of federation was considered a traitor.

Yet blame implies responsibility. The regions turned inward during the depression, and looked to the "nation." They came to terms with the federal structure and began thinking of Canada as a unit.

The long-range effects of the depression were essentially good. It forced the regions to develop new economies. Financial interests from Montreal and Boston, for instance, combined to start a large iron and steel operation in Nova Scotia, using coal from there and ore from Newfoundland.

In Central Canada, mixed farming took over the small grain farms. Mines for asbestos, nickel, and silver opened. And the burden of having to import coal to this region was relieved by the development of hydropower. Almost before the newly invented electric dynamo was complete, Canadians were harnessing their numerous waterways. As for the sawn lumber industry, now that the good timber was gone, it converted to pulpwood and newsprint production, centering around Trois Rivières.

On the Plains, research in wheat developed new strains, Red Fife and Marquis. These cut the growing season from 137 days to 105 days, lessening the chance of frost catching the wheat in the fields. And farm machinery began to appear, revolutionizing the harvesting season. British Columbia, meanwhile, began to develop lumber operations, mines, and fisheries—resources that were more stable and sure than gold.

During the years between Confederation and the turn of the century, Canada established its modern economy. It began the period with an economy based on speculation and fast money—lumber, railroads, land promotion, gold. It entered the twentieth century with a solid economy—now it was a major producer of wheat and steel. Soon it would produce more asbestos, nickel, newsprint, and hydropower than any other country in the world.

By the end of World War I, Canada had emerged as a major trading nation. In general, Canada sold to Britain and bought from the United States. No longer was the Canadian economy a pawn between Great Britain and the United States. Now the international commerce was a triangular affair among Canada, Great Britain, and the United States.

Its international politics reflected this new standing. At the time of Confederation, Canada was torn between two other more powerful countries. On the one hand, Britain always spoke for Canada at the international bargaining table. A few years after Confederation, for instance, Britain actually gave Maritime fishing rights to the United States. On the other hand, at this same time, Charles Sumner of the U.S. Senate was calling for the annexation of Canada to the United States. But by the end of World War I, Canada had shed this dependent and vulnerable status. How this change came about is a very interesting story. It reflects the fact that Canada is both one nation (Canada) and two nations (English Canada and French Canada), at the same time.

In 1896, just as the depression was lifting, the Liberals came into office. Macdonald had died in 1891, leaving the Conservatives without a strong leader. Canada had suffered through a long depression. As the economy began to recover, it seemed time for a new age. At the helm of the Liberal Party was a French Canadian named Wilfrid Laurier. And the optimistic new age, which was to last until World War I, was his.

Whereas Macdonald had been down-home, folksy, and wily, Laurier was elegant, cultivated, and a master of diplomacy—well able to hold his own with such leaders as Theodore Roosevelt. A French Canadian along the lines of George Cartier (Macdonald's partner in Confederation), Laurier's business interests were tied up with the dominant English Canadians. He believed wholeheartedly that Canada was *one* nation, and a nation with a destiny. He proclaimed that the twentieth century would be Canada's century.

But he reckoned with only one nation, Canada. He reckoned without the French Canadians. Just as Canadians were becoming conscious of themselves as a nation, so were the French Canadians becoming conscious of themselves as a nation. This had been developing ever since the execution of Riel in 1885, when the Québécois and the Métis discovered one another and united as a people. It was exacerbated when the ruling interests of Manitoba, who were oriented toward Ontario, tried to crush French language and religion in the province's schools. The controversy raged on for years. Because Laurier did not speak for them on this issue, the French Canadians needed another voice. This they found in Henri Bourassa.

The grandson of the revolutionary Papineau, the brilliant protégé of Laurier, Bourassa was more radical than his mentor, more magnetic than his grandfather. Bourassa broke with Laurier in 1905 over the Manitoba Schools question, and steadily asserted French Canadian rights thereafter. Whereas Laurier was the symbol of emerging Canadian nationality, Bourassa became the symbol of emerging French Canadian nationality. And this French Canadian nationalism had a profound effect on Canada's international position.

The crux around which Canada's independence formed was Great Britain's military operations since the turn of the century.

As the war in South Africa (the Boer War) drained Britain's resources, and as the Prussians began to build their mighty armies, Britain turned to Canada for assistance. British diplomats pressed Laurier to supply troops as their contribution to the Empire. Canada's ties to Great Britain were many, not just in commerce and trade, but in sentiment also. The question that remained unsettled, however, was exactly what was Canada's role in the Empire. According to the French Canadians, *they* were not part of Great Britain at all.

French Canada had a long tradition of pacifism. The original settlers of Canada, the Acadians, refused to fight. In Quebec the *habitants* had always resisted being drawn into wars. And even the independent Métis had favored peace until their backs were against the wall. This and the new-found French Canadian unity in the face of Riel's death and the Manitoba Schools question forged a powerful resistance to the English demands.

One newspaper summed up the general feeling with: "We French Canadians belong to one country, Canada; Canada is for us the whole world; but the English Canadians have two countries, one here and one across the sea." Under the brilliant leadership of Bourassa, the one-third of Canada's population that was French-speaking veered Canada from a course of compliance to one of independence.

Laurier, himself a French Canadian, was more conscious of it on the war issue than he was on the Manitoba Schools issue. It was a ticklish business, for Canada could not afford to offend Great Britain. Laurier played his role with great diplomatic skill. He countered Britain's pressure to send troops with an offer to take responsibility for defending Canada. And he remained firm.

Canada was thus able to get by with only a minimal contribution to the Boer War at the turn of the century. But by the time World War I began in 1914, circumstances had changed. Since 1911, Canada had a new Prime Minister, Robert Borden, a Conservative from Nova Scotia, where the political system was top-heavy with U.E. Loyalists. Then too, the magnitude of the approaching war was frightening. This was not a matter of Great Britain's grabbing territory; it could well be a question of England's survival. When war was first declared, nearly all of Canada rallied; Borden won over the Quebec clergy and even Laurier.

He did not win Bourassa though, nor the French Canadians. Very few of them volunteered. Canada did contribute, but not with French blood. Newfoundland sent 7,000 soldiers to the British armies, 4,000 of whom became casualties. Canada built up its own navy, an odd colorful fleet of sloops, trawlers, drifters, tugs, and ferries, whose main purpose was to keep open the vital shipping lines to England. And in the new British air force, a quarter of the fighters were Canadians, who showed a special aptitude for air warfare.

But even among English Canadians, there was indifference to the war after the first burst of war fever. Farmers and trade unionists particularly began to resist the war efforts. By 1916, the number of volunteers had dropped so steeply that Borden was forced to push conscription, which further turned the country against the war.

Borden's course to independence had already been set by Laurier, and despite his pro-English sympathies, Borden worked steadily toward Canda's making its own decisions. His position with Britain was that he would support the war, but Canada expected to have a voice in its destiny. It expected to have a voice in military decisions. In 1917, finally, Canada joined the Allies' top-level decision-making body, the Imperial War Cabinet, as a separate nation. And when the League of Nations was formed, Canada joined as a separate nation.

The name Dominion of Canada now stood for something. From a railroad speculator's financial scheme, Canada had become a country with many steady economies. From pockets of population on either coast, its people now spanned the continent.

From a collection of regions at odds with the "nation," it had developed an equilibrium between nation and regions. From dependence on Britain and the United States, it had grown into a major world trader. It could now be called a nation.

DEPRESSION AND WAR

ELEVEN

In the first half of the twentieth century, industrialization came into its own in Canada. And after World War I, Canada came into industrialization. During the first decade following the war, industrialization presented a spectacle of untold wealth. The second decade brought a depression more terrible and shocking than anyone could have imagined. And the third decade brought the worst war the world has ever known.

By the end of World War I, there were two major changes in Canadian society, trends that would never be reversed. The first was internal: a shift from the country to the city. In 1871, when the first Canadian census was taken, 20 percent of the population was urban. By 1920, the urban population was 56 percent. And the majority of Canada's people lived in the industrialized eastern half of the country. Halifax and Saint John, though not industrial cities, received a tremendous boost by federal improvements of their ports. Sydney on Cape Breton Island, Nova Scotia, was now a large center for coal, iron, and steel. The Saguenay region made Canada the world's largest producer of aluminum. Because of the position of the province of Quebec on the St. Lawrence, and the cheap labor French Canadians provided, the cities of Montreal and Quebec spawned numerous manufactures. Toronto was fast becoming the commercial center of Canada, edging out the slightly larger Montreal. North of Lake Erie, centered in Windsor, Ontario, were the Michigan-dominated automobile plants.

The work available in these centers drew the population from the countryside. At the same time, in western Canada, new urban centers were beginning to serve the agricultural and forest lands in transportation and commerce. Vancouver surpassed Winnipeg to become Canada's third largest city. Calgary, Alberta, was well on its way toward becoming Canada's beef capital. Edmonton, Alberta, which had first blossomed during the gold rushes, was the center for exploration of the north. Canada now had seven cities with populations of over 100,000.

The second trend after World War I was Canada's shift from Britain to the United States—both economically and politically. Up through World War I, Great Britain was the biggest investor in Canada, especially in steel and mining in the eastern regions. In 1920, Britain invested just slightly more than the United States. By 1930, the United States had pulled far ahead of Britain in Canadian investment.

The United States emerged from the war as the world's greatest power. Canada's new ties with its neighbor had a great deal to do with Canada's internal shift from rural to urban, because much of the technology for industrialization came from the United

States. So did the capital. By the 1920s, the U.S. owned one-fifth of Canadian manufacturing.

The dominant force in Canadian politics during this whole era, from the end of World War I through World War II, was William Lyon Mackenzie King of the Liberal Party. Grandson and namesake of the famous revolutionary of 1837, he had little of his forebear's fire or passion, little of what we generally think of as "natural" leadership. He often seemed confused, awkward, introverted. But behind that awkwardness lay a brilliant capacity for manipulation, an unswerving drive for power, and an unerring sense of where that power lay.

In Canada's political history, there seems to be a pattern of two types of national leaders. The first are in the tradition of John A. Macdonald, wily politicians who are masters of compromise, who manage to combine all the regions into a single nation, even if it takes underhanded politics. Then there are the politicians of Laurier's ilk, usually French Canadians, elegant masters of international diplomacy, who are more successful at representing Canada to the world than resolving regional conflicts. Mackenzie King was of the Macdonald type. He held the country together through some of its most difficult times.

Mackenzie King involved Canada in some extraordinary enterprises, for Canada would have remained undeveloped without government involvement in what most countries leave to free enterprise. It was during his administration that the federal government became directly involved in transportation. The Canadian Pacific Railway now had competition from a number of smaller railroads that staggered haphazardly across the continent. Under Mackenzie King, these were combined into one consolidated line, the Canadian National Railroad. The CNR served to open up vast areas of Canada's Plains and North. The Northwest Territories (including the districts of Mackenzie, Keewatin, and Franklin) were established in 1927.

Likewise the Canadian Broadcasting Corporation, which is

the major producer of radio and television in Canada, and the National Film Board of Canada, which leads the world in documentary films, started under Mackenzie King. Without these "Crown corporations," Canadian technology and communication might never have gotten off the ground. And they helped establish Canada's identity.

But like Macdonald, Mackenzie King tended to be expedient and manipulative. The general picture that emerges from his confused politics is one of a skilled parliamentarian rather than a leader. When on the attack, he encouraged differences among his opponents, so that they were not able to agree enough to unite against him. When attacked, his strategy was to sit with an uncomfortable, slightly astonished air—and do absolutely nothing. He pacified the provincial governments with patronage at crucial junctures, and mystified the general public with vague, contradictory, say-nothing statements. The considerable power he held for thirty years was maintained in part by his alliance with the industrialists on a national level and on the international level, by riding the coattails of the United States.

The Liberals now served the same interests and followed the same policies that had prevailed since the time of Macdonald and the Conservatives—high tariffs to protect the industries, and the subservience of all regional economies to the big business of Central Canada.

This centralization was paid for by the people of Canada. They paid for the railroads through taxes, and for tariffs by the higher prices they had to pay for goods. The Plains farmer had to take whatever price Central Canadian brokers paid for the wheat. The miner in the Maritimes, the factory worker in Montreal, the lumberjack in British Columbia—all had to take what their employers decided to pay, or do without jobs.

This state of affairs, in which most people in Canada were not represented by the Liberal/Conservatives, had led to a virtual revolution in the conditions of working people (as it did in the

United States). In the industrialized centers, this revolution took the form of trade unionism. Among farmers, it was called collectivism. Among women, it was called feminism.

The union movement started in the nineteenth century. During the 1870s, some workers in Canada had begun to demand a nine-hour day, and in 1873, their right to do so was legally sanctioned by the Trade Union Act. With the industrialization that had begun seriously in the 1890s, little craft unions had sprouted like scattered mushrooms. These were usually small local unions, composed of workers who had the same occupation—or "craft."

In the early twentieth century, a new kind of union, called a "syndicate," gained popularity in Canada. A great number of workers felt craft unions were not radical enough, and broke away to form syndicates for the mass of unskilled workers, who had no "craft." The actions of the syndicate were intensely local, short-term, based on absolutely democratic decisions by the workers themselves. This spontaneous structure suited workers who were never in one place too long—construction workers, loggers, and farm workers. So syndicalism tended to be stronger in the less centralized West than in the industrial East.

The most famous syndicate was the International Workers of the World (IWW). It was particularly strong in British Columbia, as it was on the West Coast of the United States. In Vancouver, an IWW member could always count on a bed in some worker's home until work could be found. And a Chinese-Canadian who operated a small restaurant would feed any worker who showed an IWW card. This restaurateur pronounced W as "Wobbly," and all over the North American continent, IWW members began calling themselves "Wobblies."

On the Plains, syndicalism and populism combined with regionalism into yet another form. Here the farmers began in the early 1900s organizing grain growers associations to influence wheat prices in the East. Not having the industrial weapon of strike, they utilized the populist weapon of vote. All across the Plains, small, intensely local political parties sprang into being.

The movement of both trade unionists and farmers during this first period through World War I was as much social and political as economic. The new organizations were not just asking for better pay and prices: they demanded a whole change in the social structure.

Because of this social consciousness, the union and farmer organizations became natural allies with the feminists. The sustained effort to get women the vote, on both the provincial and Dominion level, required members of the legislatures—men, in other words—to introduce bills time and time again. Most of these men were representatives of the radical workers/farmers movement, and most were socialists.

In 1918, Canadian women received the vote. This was two years before the United States, and ten years before Great Britain, passed similar legislation. Thereafter, the more militant feminists turned their energies from the women's movement, per se, into union and farm organizing. For by 1920, union and agricultural organizations were where the most dramatic changes were beginning to occur.

In 1917, the Russian Revolution had shaken the world, and the industry-labor conflict in the Western world really began to crackle. On one side was the cry, "Workers of the world, unite!" On the other side, the cry was, "Wipe out the Reds."

In 1919 came the Winnipeg General Strike. By then an urban center like cities in the East, yet Plains in character, Winnipeg labor combined unionism with syndicalism, organization with radicalism. The strike began in the metal trades and spread from union to union, then to sympathetic non-unionists. Soon the whole city was on strike. Farmers from the surrounding countryside sent in produce and dairy products. The townspeople, with the aid of the farmers, might have held out indefinitely, but the Royal Canadian Mounted Police were sent in to break the strike by force. This marked the decisive entry of the Canadian government, through the Mounties, into industrial-labor politics.

The easiest target for government intervention was the Communist Party. Although there were radical socialists in the period before World War I, the Communist Party itself did not start until 1921, when the Social Democratic Party voted itself into a "revolutionary party" after the Russian Revolution. Often characterized as "foreign subversive," most of the Communists were actually Canadian nationalists. The main purpose of their activities was not to determine international policy but to aid local causes. Their platforms called for such reforms as social security, minimum wage laws, jobs and scholarships for youth, equal rights for women—nothing that would be considered shocking or radical today. Some of their stoutest defenders were not radicals at all, but religious leaders and democrats.

Because the Communists, far from being underhanded and subversive, were the most vocal group clamoring for change, the most open about their aims and plans, they made easy targets for persecution. The fear of labor organizing became the fear of "Reds," and the brunt of the battle against unions fell on Communists. The Canadian government, unlike the United States, actually went so far as to outlaw the Communist Party several times, though public opinion always forced it to lift the ban.

In all of North America, the Communists were major contributors to the modern trade union, particularly in breaking ground and organizing. When their party first formed, unions were still in their childhood. There were the craft unions, often composed of skilled workers who regarded themselves as a sort of elite. And there were syndicates for the more radical workers who were on the bottom of the heap. For the increasing number of semi-skilled workers in the middle, however, for the masses who filled the factories and plants, there was little. Only the railroad workers and coal miners had developed strong unions. In the pulp, paper, mining, and automobile industries, there were unions that cooperated with the companies. The large industries, such as textiles, logging, packing, furniture manufacturing, sawmills, and general manufacturing, had no unions.

From the United States came the concept of "industrial" unions. Unlike craft unions, which formed around a certain skill or particular occupation, and covered only a small group, the industrial union proposed to organize the workers of all occupations within a certain industry.

Thoroughly alarmed, the industrialists fought back with everything they had. During the 1925 steelworkers' strike on Cape Breton Island, for instance, armed troops were sent from Toronto, provincial police were sent from Halifax, and the giant corporation—British Empire Steel Corporation (BESCO)—hired 400 strike-breakers of its own. When this army of several thousands converged on Sydney, there was a reign of terror. So it was in every industry, a battle all the way. But one by one through the turbulent 1920s, industries were organized.

The farmers, too, became militant during the 1920s. On the Plains, the upsurge of local parties in the 1920s was actually a widespread revolt. The form that it took in developing into long-lived, firmly entrenched political parties was unique to Canada and played a much more significant role in Canadian history than did Populism in the United States. The prophet of the Canadian movement was American-born Henry Wise Wood, who founded the popular *Grain Growers Guide* and the Grain Growers Grain Association in the early 1900s. Here too the movement was concerned with social as well as economic change. Especially influential were the Protestant fundamentalist churches; every social protest, whether to free imprisoned Communists or to support mothers with public funds, could count a number of Methodist preachers in its ranks.

The Plains people generally were against such things as protective tariffs and conscription, and for such things as women's rights and social welfare. Economically, they organized cooperatives, and then in the 1920s, great Wheat Pools—collective organizations through which farmers stored, sold, and shipped their own grain. By the end of the decade, the three Plains provinces of Alberta, Manitoba, and Saskatchewan between them owned 1,634 country elevators and 11 huge terminal elevators on the Great Lakes and Pacific Ocean, and were shipping wheat to 19 countries.

Just as startling is the strength the grass-roots political parties gained. Despite their "strictly local" base, they became provincial powers. The United Farmers of Ontario, for instance, had control of that province's government from 1919 to 1923. And in Alberta, H. W. Wood's province and "the farmer's last frontier," the United Farmers of Alberta ruled from 1921 to 1935.

This movement to power by common people in Canada was the most dramatic event of the early twentieth century. All across the Dominion, from British Columbia to Nova Scotia, the people were organizing. There was only one province in all of Canada where organization failed, and that was probably the province that needed organization most: Quebec.

Quebec remained cut off from this great movement largely because of the Catholic Church. The Church hierarchy—though not always the local priests—finally came to claim that even *strikes* were sinful. And women in Quebec did not get the vote until 1938, two decades after other provinces.

If any province needed unions, it was Quebec. The local economy was controlled by an *Anglais* elite, who were allied with the United States manufacturers. The U.S. companies in turn opened subsidiary factories, or invested heavily in partially Canadian-owned firms, in order to take advantage of the "cheap labor across the border." The cheap laborers were French Canadians.

Now the economic power that the *Anglais* had had ever since the Conquest was beginning to tell. The "economy" could be ingnored by *habitants* so long as they could quietly farm and keep to the old way of life in rural Quebec. But Quebec was no longer a rural society; the majority of its population lived in cities.

The low wages and killing hours naturally caused a good deal of unrest among the workers, especially in the 1920s, when the Québécois began to notice that workers in other places were winning better conditions for themselves. Small radical groups began forming. And the American Federation of Labor (AFL) from the United States began moving in to organize. The AFL interest in Quebec developed from the fact that U.S. companies were avoiding the wage demands of U.S. workers by seeking out cheap labor across the border.

The Church hierarchy reacted to the AFL—which could hardly be called radical, much less Communist—as though it were an invasion from Moscow. Through a hysterical campaign against ''Reds'' and ''foreigners,'' they successfully diverted the unrest into the so-called ''Catholic syndicates.'' These had little in common with the earlier syndicates such as the IWW, for these ''unions'' banned the workers' most powerful weapon, the strike. This did little to help the workers themselves, who continued to be ''cheap labor.''

The peculiar combination of suppressive forces in Quebec created a pressure for popular expression. French Canadians were torn between their class, which was poor; their nationalism, which was based on a rich heritage; and their religion, which was involved in every economic and political part of their lives. The combination of virulent anti-communism and nationalism led—as it did in many countries at this time—to fascism.

We find this a little shocking today, considering what fascism became under Hitler. But every movement in its early stages has elements which represent common people, and every movement carries the seed of evil. The appeal of fascism lay in its nationalism, which is a rallying point for many oppressed people, its reverence for unspoiled country life, and its patriotic ideals of homeland. Fascism gained some popularity in almost every Western country (including the United States) during the 1930s. And if two such different peoples as the Italians and the Germans could find meaning in it, the deeply nationalistic Québécois could also.

In 1929, the Great Depression struck, and all the social elements in Canada—the alliance of government and industry, the economic dependence of workers and farmers, trade unionism, communism, new political parties, and fascism—were intensified by the worst financial disaster in history. In the world market, countries stopped buying imported goods. The raw resources by which Canada had held its place in the world economy were no longer in demand, and industries based on lumber and pulp, commercial fishing, and mining closed down. The Canadian wheat market collapsed.

The manufacturers were the most fortunate: their assets were not worthless "paper" as were the financiers', but solid buildings and equipment. They managed to keep prices up by laying off workers, cutting wages, and increasing hours. During some of the worst years of the Depression, the corporations showed rising profits, while at the same time wages were dropping.

But for most of Canada, so long dependent on the export of raw resources, the Depression was catastrophic. As the lumber, fishing, and mining industries closed down, thousands of workers were thrown out of jobs. They flocked to the cities looking for work and there found thousands of factory workers unemployed.

On the Plains the situation was, if it could be, worse. As the wheat market collapsed, the Wheat Pools were rendered ineffective, and the farmers could not sell their grain for anything near a decent price. But that was just the beginning. The first shock of the wheat collapse was followed by a terrible drought, which lasted more or less for ten years. The wheat shriveled, the cattle died, the wind picked up the dirt and blew it in raging dust storms which could be seen for hundreds of miles.

Today if people are out of work, or if women with children

are left with no income, they can at least find temporary means through unemployment insurance or public relief. In those days there were no unemployment benefits, and relief was provided only on a small scale by cities and private charities. Desperate, the people looked for some remedy.

In 1930, Mackenzie King took a five-year breather from his reign of nearly thirty years. The new Prime Minister, thanks to the support of worried eastern industrialists, was R. B. Bennett, a multi-millionaire Conservative. Bennett's blustery campaign promised tariff protection for industry and jobs for workers; for the farmers, he would "blast our way into the markets of the world." His first "emergency" action once in office was to raise the protective tariffs. That was about as far in his program as he went.

The rest of Bennett's term is notable mainly for his trying to control the people with dictatorial tactics. One of his first orders of business was to outlaw the Communist Party. He built the Royal Canadian Mounted Police into a spy and surveillance organization to suppress radical activities. And perhaps worst of all, he herded 40,000 young people into what amounted to forced-labor camps.

During the Depression, there were an estimated half million people between the ages of fifteen and twenty-four who had no jobs and little hopes of getting any. In most families college was out of the question, and in many, young people could not burden their families by staying home and finishing high school. Thousands of them roamed back and forth across the country, looking for work, catching rides in boxcars, sleeping in the open. Bennett's answer was "youth camps," where the youths were housed and fed under miserable conditions and made to work on road-building or brush-clearing projects. This experience made a great number of youths very radical very quickly.

In British Columbia the young people eventually reached the point where they could take no more. The broke out of the camps and were taken in by thousands of Vancouver families. The mothers of the city marched 5,000 strong in protest, calling for abolition of the "slave camps." The youths themselves organized a protest march, which they hoped would carry them all the way from the Pacific Coast to Ottawa. Nearly 800 of them set out from Vancouver. "Wait till they feel the nip of frost up in the mountains," the newspapers cackled, "and they'll be glad to get back to camp."

But no. The young people, many of them children, crossed the mountain wilderness of interior British Columbia, crossed the great Rockies, crossed half of the Plains, covering over a thousand miles. And when they reached Regina, their numbers had *doubled*. They would have made it to Ottawa. But at Regina, the Bennett government sent armed troops against the young people. The march was stopped, but the public concern it caused did, in turn, put an end to the "youth camps."

Except for such negative actions, the Bennett government did little to cope with the crisis. The cities, towns, and private charities were finally overwhelmed by the sheer numbers asking for help. Then the provinces tried to shoulder the responsibility, which severely strained their resources. One result of the lack of Dominion responsibility, however, was that the provinces emerged from the Depression with much more power than before.

Meanwhile, people got along somehow. The farmers, for instance, supported one another so strongly that when the sheriff came to auction off someone's property, the farmers refused to bid against each other. The farm would end up being sold for $20 or so, and returned to its dispossessed owner.

Trade unionism likewise proceeded apace, as the workers grew more radical. Industrial unions made fast gains on the more conservative AFL craft unions, and soon the United States Congress of Industrial Organization (CIO) was affiliating these industrial unions, competing with the AFL as an "international" union.

During the time the Communist Party was illegal, two very important parties began on the Plains. One of these was the Social Credit Party which took over control of Alberta from the United Farmers in 1935. This party had elements of both socialism (it pledged to pay every adult $25 a month) and fascism (it was anti-Semitic). The other "western" party was the Co-operative Commonwealth Federation (CCF). It began on the Plains, but soon had a great deal of support in Ontario, where Methodist social conscience was strong.

In Quebec, another party emerged which was to have an important role in Canada's future. That was the *Union Nationale,* a party which presented itself as highly nationalistic. It was led by Maurice Duplessis, whose philosophy could be more easily classified as fascist than as nationalistic. For all his talk of nationalism, Duplessis was so involved with U.S. industrialists that he practically sold Quebec to the *Anglais* and Yankees before he was through. After he gained control of the provincial government in 1936, he arrested the more radical unionists, often without charges, padlocking their houses, and instituting a spy and surveillance system in which the police were used to watch over citizens.

Then came World War II. For a time, when Hitler first came to power in 1933, some in the industrialized nations hoped he would check the power of the Soviet Union. In Canada itself, Quebec's Duplessis and several of his business cronies began negotiations to lease Germany a naval base on Anticosti Island, right in the middle of the St. Lawrence. Then Hitler attacked Poland, and Britain and France finally realized that he would turn on them next. Industrialists and Communists, Canadians and *Canadiens* alike finally united against the Nazis, and "fascism," at least for a time, became a hated word.

Over a million men and women, most of them volunteers, joined the Canadian armed forces. Perhaps the most distinguished unit was the Royal Canadian Air Force, which accounted for nearly half of the 42,000 Canadians killed. And once again, the

Canadian navy, centered in Halifax, was destined to keep open the crucial northern shipping lines to Europe. There were many more small ships than large fighting ships, and these little boats ran into some terrible battles with submarines and aircraft.

The Canadian economy meanwhile had swelled to meet war needs. Manufactures multiplied, agricultural production increased in value by 60 percent. Canada was able to give more than $4 billion in goods to its allies. The Dominion emerged from the war in fairly good shape. Industry was particularly favored, for it had expanded considerably, and the war profits were huge.

But after thirty years of tumultuous change, boom, depression, and war on a scale the world had never known, the nation and its parts were no closer than before. The strong regional splits, natural to Canada to begin with and increased during the Bennett administration, would not be mended overnight. Quebec was now firmly in the hands of Duplessis' *Union Nationale*. It had been further alienated over conscription, which Mackenzie King managed to slip through Parliament. Social Credit still held Alberta. In Saskatchewan, the CCF had taken hold with equal certainty, and was determined to push reform legislation.

The one encouragement to centralization was the case of Newfoundland. The Depression hit Newfoundland harder than anywhere except perhaps the Plains, principally because the people there were so poor to begin with. Whereas in the rest of Canada, this industry or that market collapsed, in Newfoundland's case, Newfoundland collapsed. Appealing to Britain for help, the island was taken over by the British government in 1934 and slowly helped toward recovery.

Then with the war, Newfoundland's strategic position made it a North Atlantic focus of British, Canadian, and United States armed power. Suddenly there was more employment than people, and the island knew some of the most prosperous days ever. The end of the war, however, threw Newfoundland back on its own economy, which was insufficient. With England so sorely wounded, there was little sense in appealing to it. So New-foundland, the last province, was left no choice but to join the Confederation. It finally took its place in the Dominion in 1949.

But given Newfoundland's history and geography, no New-foundlander would call her/himself a "Canadian." Likewise, modern-day residents of Baddeck, for example, call themselves Baddeckers or Capers (for Cape Breton Island) first, and Nova Scotians or Maritimers second. They would not think of calling themselves Canadians.

Yet a strong Canadian *nation* would be necessary in the new post-war world. It was a world in which the two greatest powers in history—the United States and the Soviet Union—were squaring off for Cold War. Still under Mackenzie King, Canada first fell into line behind the United States. McCarthyism and the Korean War came to Canada, and missile bases, too. It would be easy to think of Canada as a "little brother," tagging along.

But that is not how it turned out. Canada had a much larger role to play.

STRUGGLE FOR IDENTITY

TWELVE

During the two decades between the end of World War II and the cultural revolution of the late 1960s, Canada continued to struggle for its own identity. This period began with a federal-provincial conference to settle the conflict between nation and region, once and for all. But by the end of this period, Alberta and British Columbia were speaking of secession, and there was so much unrest in Quebec that thousands of federal troops were sent in to occupy Montreal.

Likewise, internationally Canada began this period looking forward to a close and profitable relationship with the United States. But by the late 1960s, Canada had withdrawn so far from its neighbor that on both sides of the border there were whispers of economic reprisals by the United States.

So nothing was settled; nothing ever has been in Canada. The conflicts between the "nation" and its parts, and with the nations with whom it trades, have formed Canada. Perhaps these conflicts will never be solved. Perhaps it is the conflict rather than its solution that is Canada's identity.

After World War II, and through much of the 1950s, Canada followed the United States into a boom period. Because of this, the inherent federal-provincial conflict took on the character of fighting over pieces of the post-war pie. There was a lot of money to be made in deals with the United States; the question was, would most of it go to the national government or the provinces? As it turned out, there was plenty to go around.

In 1946, oil was discovered by Imperial Oil at Leduc, south of Edmonton, Alberta. In 1947, Imperial Leduc No. 1 blew in, and by 1957, Canada was producing 170 million barrels per day. In the early 1950s, a pipeline was constructed for crude oil, from Edmonton to Sarnia, Ontario, 1,765 miles, then the longest pipeline in the world.

Vast iron deposits were discovered in eastern Quebec and Labrador. Soon mineral and forest products surpassed even wheat as exports. Wheat-growing, meanwhile, was at its best, earning $450 million in wheat exports in 1952. Even Canada's industries gained importance in world terms; stimulated by the recent war, yet undamaged like Britain's, they converted easily to peacetime production. Construction and manufacturing boomed.

In the midst of all this good fortune, Canada decided to create a "national culture," just as Macdonald had created a "nation." Two decades before, the federal government had started just that very thing with several national boards—the Canadian Broadcasting Corporation, the National Museum, and the National Film Board. Now in 1949, the government decided to promote the always-neglected arts more energetically, and it appointed the Royal Commission on National Development in the Arts, Letters, and Sciences. It was chaired by Vincent Massey, the distinguished chancellor of the University of Toronto, and included members from several regions. The result of the staggering research done by this small commission is known as the Massey Report, issued in 1951. Some of its recommendations were: the promotion and control of television by the federal government; federal aid to universities; and the establishment of the Canada Council to give grants to institutions and individuals involved with the arts.

In the 1950s also, the federal government became involved in what is loosely known as "welfare," or "social services." It proposed the introduction of national old age pensions and health plans. Having left the responsibility for such things to the provinces during the recent Depression, the federal government now proposed to take charge, in return for a certain share in provincial taxes, which had been allotted to the provinces by the British North American Act.

Even the best of times could not veil for very long the split that has always existed between the nation and the regions. In the midst of prosperity, both the federal and provincial governments were determined to gain control of the provincial economies. All the optimism of the early 1950s broke up when the question of university grants, national health plans, and especially natural resources came to the fore.

The provinces were feeling independent. The maverick Social Credit Party still controlled Alberta, which had been transformed from a province of depressed farmers to a land of the new oil-rich. The provincial government and financiers were involved in selling off Albertan oil to United States corporations. Encroachments by the Canadian federal government threatened these profits. In British Columbia, Social Credit (a more liberal variety than Alberta's) put W. A. C. Bennett into power in 1952. The party there was still in its fledgling stage, and it took on the highly personal coloring of Bennett, who welded together a tough, long-lasting government. He and the Social Credit Party completely identified with British Columbia, not Canada. Bennett wanted as little interference from the federal government as possible, especially because he was interested in selling off British Columbian timber to U.S. lumberers.

Saskatchewan, where the libertarian CCF still held sway, was years ahead of the federal government in social legislation: it had socialized medicine, for instance, long before the federal government made its own proposal, which the province regarded as superfluous. In Newfoundland, the popular Joey Smallwood governed the province under the same Liberal Party that now controlled the federal government. But he and Newfoundland were almost as independent as, and had more personal style than, W. A. C. Bennett and British Columbia. Quebec and the Maritimes both had old regimes—French Canadian in one case, U.E. Loyalist in the other. The governments in these two areas were firmly entrenched. They had no intention of handing over provincial powers on social legislation and taxation to the federal government. If the federal government had so much money to throw around, they asked, why did it not turn income taxes over to the provinces, or give them the money directly and let the provinces give it away? All of the provinces were suspicious.

But the most consistent gadfly to centralization was Maurice Duplessis, who was again premier of Quebec during the 1950s. His rule in Quebec was still the rule of a dictator. He was, as one journalist wrote, "master under God" in Quebec.

Under the cover of Canadian nationalism, he made deals with United States corporations, which virtually gave away Quebec's new resource, iron. He encouraged U.S. companies to come to Canada with the promise of cheap labor. He turned down federal money for universities and held up funds for social legislation, certainly at a cost in education and health to the *Canadiens*. His regime was rocked by scandal after corrupt scandal, until even the middle class of Quebec turned against him. If he had not died in 1959, he most surely would have been ousted.

Why was he elected by the *Canadien* people again and again? Because the part of him that was not opportunist was nationalist. He was the only strong voice for French Canadian culture. Again and again he said, Quebec is *not* like other provinces. Its race is a founding race; its people are like no others in Canada.

For this reason also, the Catholic Church, which can be charged with keeping the *Canadiens* in economic chains, was supported by most of the French-speaking population. In the face of *Anglais* domination, which threatened their very language, who else but the Church and Duplessis spoke for *Canadien* culture?

Besides, what Duplessis was doing on the provincial level was essentially no different from what was happening on the federal level. The argument over natural resources was not over practically giving them away, for short-term profit, to the United States. The argument was over who would get those short-term profits. The federal government was just as eager to latch onto the United States boom as were the provincial premiers.

Many of the differences between Liberal and Conservative were disappearing. The Liberals tended to support more government intervention in business, which lost them the small business vote. But in return they gained the favor of the big corporations—mainly because big corporations seem to benefit from government intervention.

In 1948, Mackenzie King finally retired, shortly before his death. He left behind a strong Liberal Party structure that survived him by a decade, under the do-nothing leadership of Louis St. Laurent. St. Laurent followed his predecessor's policies of centralization and further involvement with the United States.

The provincial governments continuously raised the charge of "centralization" against the federal government. But despite their clamor and resistance, centralization was a fact. Industrialization always centralizes power: its form is not the free and open market, but the monopoly. Its basis is not the independent farmer or fisher tied to the land or sea, but the urban worker who is so dependent on the corporation that he or she will move thousands of miles every few years, for work.

Centralization was a fact in industry and commerce, where corporations and conglomerates quickly took the place of individual or family-owned companies. It was a fact in labor relations, where the affiliate of craft unions combined with the affiliate of industrial unions in 1956 to form the Canadian Labour Congress (CLC), roughly comparable to the AFL-CIO in the United States.

Centralization was a fact in agriculture where, with modern machinery, nutrients, and hybrids, a single farmer could cultivate as much as 1,000 acres on the Plains. And it was even a fact in religion, where three of the largest Protestant churches outside of the Anglican Church—Presbyterian, Methodist, and Congregational—joined together as the United Church of Canada.

The centralization of Canadian society made possible some remarkable projects for Canadian development. The great oil pipeline from Edmonton to Ontario was such a project. And the Trans-Canada Highway, which by 1962 would span the entire continent, was also started in the 1950s. But the most dramatic project was the St. Lawrence Seaway.

Canada wanted to build this waterway so ships could reach the Great Lakes from the St. Lawrence. For a time, it was too ambitious a project for Canada alone, but the United States responded listlessly when asked to join. Finally Canada decided it could manage by itself. Then the United States changed its mind. Begun in 1954, the Seaway was inaugurated in 1959 by Queen Elizabeth and President Eisenhower.

With its 27-foot draught, the Seaway is deep enough for ocean traffic. Its locks can hold a ship 730 feet long and 75 feet wide. The really gigantic ships are usually not ocean freighters but "lakers," which travel only on the Lakes and the St. Lawrence, taking cargo from one end to the other. With the Seaway, North

America now has direct ocean access to the heart of the continent, for this water route extends over 2,000 miles from the Atlantic to Chicago and Duluth. It was a magnificent joint feat, and at the time the two countries undertook it, it seemed to seal their joint future.

After World War II, Canada had made a definite turn away from Britain and toward the United States. This was accompanied by a rise in U.S. investment that was more pronounced than in the period following World War I. By 1954, U.S. investors had bet on Canada to the tune of nearly $10 billion. Soon the United States owned or controlled most of Canada's oil, gas, rubber, and automobile production; a majority of its manufacturing, nickel, iron ore, asbestos, and aluminum productions; and over half of its pulp and paper industry. For the time being, Canada saw only the short-range profits and ignored the future.

Likewise, Canada adopted the politics of the United States, not only for economic reasons and because the government was U.S.-oriented. It was also because at that time the world image of the United States was one of the guardian of liberty. So much has happened since then that we tend to forget that Fidel Castro, like Mao Tse-tung and Ho Chi Minh before him, naïvely turned first to the United States for help and to the Communist countries only when he was rejected. The aura of Free World idealism hung over the United States.

Canada supported the international policies of the United States, following the U.S. in 1949 into the North Atlantic Treaty Organization, a mutual defense pact which also includes a number of European nations. And in 1950, it followed the United States into the Korean War, a move the Canadian government felt was justified because the troops were sent under the auspices of the United Nations. And besides, the United States, now under President Harry Truman, had offered Canada $1 billion in defense contracts. Canada followed the United States step by step, for nearly three years, right up to the point when Truman made a reference to using the atom bomb in Korea. That shook both Canada and Britain out of their complacency. From then on, they worked for a cease-fire.

The unbreakable bonds that St. Laurent's government intended for Canada and the United States never really formed. When the St. Lawrence Seaway construction began in 1954, Eisenhower was able to write cheerfully of "uniting the destinies of Canada and the United States." By the time the Seaway actually opened in 1959, however, there was none of this effusiveness from either side. And Fidel Castro, as well as Queen Elizabeth and President Eisenhower, was a guest in Montreal. Following U.S. foreign policy straight down the line did not seem to agree with Canada's national character.

A very strong part of Canada's true national character (as opposed to the "national" character as St. Laurent interpreted it) is pacifist. This has its historical basis in the refusal of French Canadians to bear arms and in the pacifist beliefs of many of the immigrant groups. It has its economic basis in the fact that Canada is a trader. By 1960, Canada ranked fifth among the world's trading nations, and income from trade alone provided one-fifth of the national wealth. Traders usually do not like war, for it interferes with business. During the colonial days, for instance, fur traders in Montreal and Albany consistently kept contact with each other and urged their governments to stop fighting.

Canada began to take its role in the United Nations very seriously, and was especially active on the Disarmament Commission. Its first major success was in 1956, when Egypt nationalized the Suez Canal, and was almost immediately invaded by Israel and by troops from Britain and France. It was a bad blunder on the part of Britain, and both the United States and Canada were appalled. The United States wanted immediate withdrawal, but the situation was too delicate for such an impulsive move.

Canada, in the person of international mediator Lester Pearson, found just the right solution—a peace-keeping force, the

United Nations Emergency Force, to police the area. Then Britain and France could leave and let the Israelis and Arabs solve their own problems. For his impressive performance, Pearson received the Nobel Prize for Peace in 1957. And by resisting both U.S. and British foreign policy in this case, Canada received the status of a "middle" nation, politically between East and West. The "middle" is an altogether excellent place for a trader to be.

Canada's first enthusiasm for trade with the United States had faded some by now. The United States was no longer a market for Canadian wheat because it had surpluses of its own. And Canada had every intention of dealing with the Communist countries which did want its wheat. This the United States could not prevent, though it caused some bad feeling. Then in 1958, Canadian newspapers gave big coverage to the fact that a Canadian automobile manufacturer had been forbidden by its U.S. parent company to ship to the People's Republic of China. Canada, of course, challenged the U.S. control, and continued to trade with countries with which the U.S. disagreed politically.

Likewise domestically, Canada found the boom euphoria fading. Social concepts had not kept pace with the headlong industrialization. The majority of Canadians did not share the great profits of the boom.

In 1965, the University of Toronto Press published a book by John Porter, *The Vertical Mosaic,* which shocked Canada. It was a socio-economic study, ambitious in scope, which examined the nation as a whole in terms of its power structure—mostly from data collected during the 1950s.

Contrary to the popular image of Canada as "classless" or "middle-class," Porter showed that Canada had a very rigid class structure. At the top, the economy was controlled by a small number of people with a great deal of power. This was true in banking, business, government, and even religion. And in these elites, there were no women, no Jews, no Native Peoples, no ethnic minorities, and with the exception of the Catholic Church in

Quebec, no Catholics or French Canadians. Having assumed economic power from the day they arrived, wealthy British Canadians preferred, naturally enough, not to share it.

The situation put them on top of the economic heap; they enjoyed not only a higher, but a *much* higher, standard of living than anyone else in Canada. At the bottom of the list were the Native Peoples, the Indians and Innuit. Not too much better off than the Native Peoples were the French Canadians. During the 1950s, Porter claimed further, most Canadians, no matter what their ethnic background, were not middle class but poor. This situation would change: the discrepancy between rich and poor was too great.

The "nationalistic" policies of the St. Laurent government finally broke on the issue of the longest pipeline yet. This pipeline would transport Canada's natural gas to the United States in huge quantities. Just becoming aware of their natural resources' long-range values, Canadians were indignant. The political conflict it raised in Parliament was so serious that, while the pipeline did go through, it cost Prime Minister St. Laurent his office in the next election.

The man who took Canada by storm in 1956 and 1957 was John G. Diefenbaker, the son of a German immigrant from Saskatchewan. A Conservative of the populist type, Diefenbaker was the first "western" Prime Minister, and furthermore someone who identified with the "third peoples." Unfortunately, he was largely ignorant of the French Canadians. Charmed enough to vote Conservative for the first time since Riel's execution, the *Canadiens* soon began to fall away. Nor could Diefenbaker get any real economic or social programs started.

He did set an important precedent by appointing to high government offices the first Native Indian and the first Ukrainian. For his Secretary of State, he appointed Ellen Fairclough, the first woman to hold a Cabinet post. He also was influential in getting South Africa removed from the Commonwealth because of its pol-

icy of *apartheid*. But his most trenchant stand was taken on nuclear weapons.

In 1957, the Canadian government signed up for Washington's joint defense plan called NORAD. The United States had already established the Distant Early Warning (DEW) Line of radar
in Canada's north country. Conscious that Canada had a neighbor
(the U.S.S.R.) on the other side of the North Pole, as well as a
neighbor to the south, the United States wanted to plant nuclear
missiles in the Arctic. The United States supplied Canada with
Bomarc missiles, for which Canada was expected to supply nuclear warheads.

Two years later, Diefenbaker still had not equipped the missiles with warheads. He managed to stall and stave off U.S. pressure until the Cuban missile crisis of late 1962. Then he delayed
supporting the United States until the time for action had passed;
he also refused to allow U.S. planes to fly over Canada during the
crisis. The United States was of course thoroughly angered by this
time, and the pressure became intense. Still Diefenbaker held out.
But because of his stand, he lost the support of his Conservative
Party and fell in the next election.

The new Prime Minister, who served from 1963 to 1968,
was Nobel Prize winner Lester B. Pearson. As adept as he was in
international affairs, Pearson had little feeling for or interest in
domestic politics. His government was colorless, predictable, and
marked by a series of scandals, none of which were very colorful
either. By the time he resigned, the scene of political action had
shifted from national government; the action was on a provincial
level.

New politicians emerged during the 1960s, and not from the
tired Conservative-Liberal establishment of national politics, but
from the tinderbox of Quebec. They were politicians bred in the
1950s, people such as the erratic Pierre Vallières from the Montreal slums and the suave Pierre Trudeau from the tiny minority of

wealthy French Canadians. History would bring these two very different men together in a dramatic way.

Raised in dire poverty under the Duplessis regime, Pierre Vallières had a confused and frustrated childhood. But his unquestionable brilliance got him through school under the Church, then college. He became a bank clerk and was miserable. Then he worked for *La Presse,* French Canada's largest daily newspaper, and despised it. He went to Paris. But the sophisticated French did not care about the social problems of Quebec, which they considered backward and provincial. Vallières came to realize that change would depend on drastic action by the Québécois themselves. He returned to Montreal and became a "separatist," a person who advocated Quebec as a separate country from Canada.

Pierre Trudeau's background was as fortunate as Vallières's was tortured. Born into a wealthy French Canadian family, Trudeau took his law degree in Montreal. He studied at Harvard, then in Paris, then London. In 1948, he began a two years' journey around the world, in the course of which he unintentionally found himself in almost every world conflict of the time. The Arabs mistook him for an Israeli spy and arrested him; in Shanghai, he was forced to flee when Mao's revolutionaries took the city.

Back in Montreal, Trudeau emerged politically, for the first time, as a supporter of the asbestos miners in a Quebec strike. He founded a magazine, *Cité Libre,* which raised opposition to the corruption of the Duplessis and St. Laurent administrations, and he taught at the Université de Montréal.

In French Canada's universities, there were two different views of Quebec's problems. One group blamed English-speaking Canadians. The other blamed the French Canadians themselves, claiming that if Quebec were to solve its problems, it must throw off the outdated controls of the Church and Duplessis, and prepare to live in the same modern world as the English Canadians. The first line of thought led to separatism; the second to reform.

In 1959, Duplessis died, and the lid he had held so tightly blew off. All of the despair and resignation of the people, who knew neither whom to blame nor whom to believe, came to the fore. The separatist movement began to swell in the early 1960s and spawned a radical separatist group, *Front de Libération Québécois* (FLQ), which advocated nothing short of revolution and terrorism. The most eloquent voice of the FLQ was the young man who had emerged from the muddy slums of Montreal, Pierre Vallières. And although the FLQ itself was small, the majority of French Canadians polled during this time favored separatism.

It was just the moment for some dynamic new politicism to bring reform and unite Canada nationally. Trudeau decided to enter national politics with the Liberal Party. He left for Ottawa, turning his magazine *Cité Libre* over to Vallières. Perhaps he was trying to channel the separatist movement into "constructive" lines. But Vallières was not diverted. Within a decade these two men would represent opposing sides in a violent national conflict.

In the meantime, provincial reform was moving Quebec out of the Dark Ages. In 1960, a solid reformer, Jean Lesage, swept into office as Premier of Quebec. He nationalized the hydroelectric companies in Quebec, took education out of the hands of the Church, and demanded separate status for Quebec. He insisted that Quebec be allowed to exchange freely with other nations, especially in matters of culture and education. His government never achieved stability, and in 1966, he lost to the party of Daniel Johnson. But he had ushered in the so-called "quiet revolution."

Daniel Johnson, despite his name, was a true French Canadian, and he took up with the federal government where Lesage left off. He demanded a "state of Quebec" and turned to France. He met with Charles de Gaulle and made specific arrangements for cultural and educational exchange.

In 1967 in Montreal, Canada's centennial celebration was observed in the stunning Universal Exposition, or "Expo 67." The

province of Quebec, though it must have shared some pride in
Expo 67, refrained from participating in the opening ceremonies.
The millions of visitors of Expo 67 were greeted with slogans
scrawled on city walls: *"Visitez les slums!"* ("Visit the Slums!")
and *"Cent ans d'injustice!"* ("A Hundred Years of Injustice!").
As usual, French Canada was becoming conscious of its nationality at the same time Canada was becoming aware of its own.

Perhaps Quebec merely wanted to celebrate the Centennial in
its own way. It had cause for celebration when General de Gaulle,
like Queen Elizabeth, came to visit Expo 67. Speaking before
millions of cheering Québécois, he let out a cry that nearly gave
Ottawa a collective heart attack: *"Vive le Québec libre!"* (Long
live free Quebec!").

Soon after the Centennial, Pearson resigned and Pierre Trudeau made one of the fastest entrances onto the world political
stage ever known. But in terms of Canadian history, it was time
for him. Like the elegant Laurier in the early part of the century,
he was due to preside over the new feeling of Canadian nationalism. Both were capable of holding their own in world politics.
Both tended to put Canadian nationalism before strictly French
Canadian nationalism. The public found him colorful and compelling.

But a few months after he was inaugurated in 1968, several
of the stronger separatist parties merged into the *Parti Québécois.*
The separatist movement seemed to be getting stronger rather than
weaker. And it put Trudeau in an uncomfortable position. On the
one hand, he was criticized by his own people for opposing separatism. On the other hand, it would be political suicide for him to
encourage it. He knew the rules of the game. Provincial premiers
such as Duplessis, Lesage, and Johnson have to fight any tinge of
Canadianism and continuously defend Quebec independence. But
Prime Ministers such as Laurier and Trudeau could afford no
tinge of *Canadien* nationalism.

The avowed terrorist FLQ in the meantime had kept up a

steady (but not particularly deadly) stream of terrorist activities. The *Front* was composed of a number of cells, each with a few members. Often members of one cell did not know members in other cells, and each cell acted independently with no centralized leadership. On October 5, 1970, the *Libération* cell of the FLQ kidnapped a British trade commissioner stationed in Montreal, James Cross. The event was orderly, well-planned, and the group disappeared into Montreal. This was Trudeau's first crisis; the world was watching.

The group first negotiated with the Quebec government. Daniel Johnson had died suddenly and been replaced (so as to avoid a recurrence of the de Gaulle episode) by Trudeau's Liberal candidate Robert Bourassa. Then after five days of tentative contact, it came out that Bourassa had no authority to negotiate with the kidnappers; he had merely been a "front" for Trudeau, stalling for time. Trudeau had no intention of negotiating. There was a good deal of public support for the FLQ group, though, and Trudeau was beginning to sweat.

He was saved by a second kidnapping, this time of a popular Quebec politician and journalist, Pierre Laporte. The FLQ *Chenier* cell that kidnapped him was neither as responsible, nor as sophisticated, nor as socially minded as the *Libération* cell of the FLQ. The *Chenier* cell would end up killing Laporte. The *Libération* cell would manage to evade the intensive police search for two months, releasing Cross in exchange for free passage out of the country.

But in the meantime Trudeau was helpless. The police were stymied. And with the eyes of the world on this new untried Prime Minister, he had to set a firm image. His answer, on October 16, 1970, was to invoke the War Measures Act, proclaiming a "state of apprehended insurrection." Then he sent 6,000 troops into Montreal.

The War Measures Act is similar to such measures in other countries. Essentially, it suspends civil liberties during wartime and gives the government sweeping powers to arrest and detain private citizens. But in other countries, such acts cease to exist after the war is over. In Canada, it continues to hover in the background and can be proclaimed during times of peace. Over 500 Québécois were arrested without charges. Nor were they allowed legal counsel, bail, or trial. Quebec considered itself—and essentially it was—an occupied country.

By early 1971, it was all over. Laporte was dead in retaliation for the War Measures. His kidnappers were arrested. Cross was free, as were *his* kidnappers. The other provinces were "fed up" with radical demands specifically and Quebec in general. The Québécois themselves wanted peace and order. Finally in April, the act was phased out. Quebec and Canada set about healing their wounds.

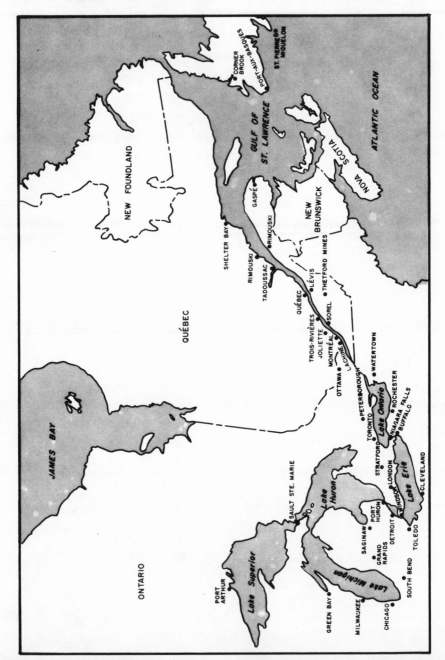

The St. Lawrence Seaway permits ships to ply their way to ports on the Great Lakes that are as much as a thousand miles inland. (*Dianna Gilmore*)

The Trans-Canada Highway, cut deep into the mountainside of British Columbia.
(*Canadian Government Travel Bureau*)

An ocean-going ship makes its way through one of the locks on the St. Lawrence Seaway. (*Canadian Government Travel Bureau*)

President Franklin D. Roosevelt of the U.S., Prime Minister Winston Churchill of Great Britain, and Canada's Prime Minister William Mackenzie King confer in Quebec during World War II. (*Canadian National Film Board*)

President Dwight D. Eisenhower and Canadian Prime Minister John Diefenbaker sign a treaty governing the use of the waters of the Columbia River Basin in 1961. (*Canadian Consulate-General, New York*)

The dome of the U.S. Pavilion built for Montreal's Expo '67. It was later converted into an aviary and garden as part of the "Man and His World" exhibition in 1970 and then into an exhibit of U.S. handicrafts under the sponsorship of the Smithsonian Institution. (*Canadian Government Travel Bureau*)

A modern apartment complex in Montreal incorporates the plans of several of Canada's top designers. (*Canadian Government Travel Bureau*)

Pierre Elliott Trudeau was Canada's Prime Minister from 1968 to 1979. (*Cavouk*)

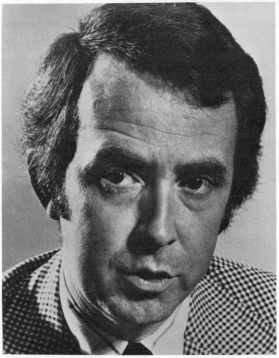

Prime Minister Joe Clark, whose Progressive Conservative Party won the 1979 general election. (*Canadian Consulate-General, New York*)

The Pickering Generating Station, near Toronto, which is to have a capacity of over four million kilowatts. (*Atomic Energy of Canada*)

Canada's dual culture is evident in this French/English street sign. (*Information Canada*)

ART AS A VITAL FORCE

THIRTEEN

While international maneuvering and internal strife were characterizing Canadian politics, Canadian art was emerging as a vital force for the first time in history. Some of the Native Peoples—particularly the Innuit and the Pacific Coast Indians—had highly developed art forms within the contexts of their respective cultures. Aside from traditional or folk art, however, art in Canada has little history before the twentieth century.

Canada was a colonial territory for nearly a hundred years after the United States declared its independence. After it was confederated in 1867, the new country was spoken for by Britain, bullied by the United States, ignored by France, and fractured by differences among its own peoples. Before the twentieth century, Canada was not really a nation on its own, and so it is only in this century that its own Canadian culture has been developing. It has done so in a most unusual manner.

The French Canadian claim that Canada is not one nation but two, French-speaking and English-speaking, is completely justified by the development of Canadian art. In general, English-speaking artists have sought to express the totality of Canada, and to define "Canada," artistically. To French-speaking artists, "Canada" more often than not means *"Anglais."* They are more interested in "aesthetics" than "Canada," and more interested in finding new techniques from Paris or New York than in defining the Canadian landscape. What is interesting, what is *Canada* in fact, is the effect these two points of view have had on one another.

English art during the eighteenth and nineteenth centuries, which English-speaking artists in Canada strove to imitate, was not equal to the Canadian environment. In the New World, everything was vast and magnificent, and the genteel landscapes of England provided only a puny technique for expressing it. Confronted with this problem, the English-speaking artists floundered.

Then the French-speaking artists, who cared less about expressing Canada than about the latest techniques from Paris, discovered French Impressionism and imported it to Canada. Suddenly the English-speaking artists had the medium they needed, and "Canadian" art was off and running.

The first "national" movement emerged after World War I with the self-proclaimed Group of Seven. The principal inspiration for the Group was Tom Thomson (1877–1917), who was passionately in love with Canada and spent most of his time in the wilderness of Ontario. His paintings of the woods and water captured the Canadian landscape as it never had been before—and may very well never be again. But just as he was mastering his art, he drowned in the wilds of Ontario.

The Group of Seven announced themselves in 1920, followed Thomson's lead, and committed themselves to the Canadian bold design and strong colors. The Group lasted until 1933, through several changes in membership. None of the Group ever equaled Thomson. The flavor of the Group, however, has survived among artists such as Charles Comfort, Kenneth Lochhead, and Jean-Paul Lemieux, who have proved better artists than those in the Group. It has in fact become a Canadian "style": simple design, large spaces.

The Group's fervent nationalism ended up restricting the development of Canadian art. The "national" movement's own forms had come from Europe in the beginning, but once they were established, they resisted any change. When it tried to exclude other new forms in the 1930s, the Group broke up.

Artists in French Canada had never really accepted the dictates of the Group. The Montreal painters, for instance, claimed that painting was not a matter of patriotism but of aesthetics. They followed developments in Paris and New York very closely, while English Canada stubbornly stuck to its landscapes. Once the hold of the Group dissolved, French Canadians ushered in the new Abstract forms. And once again, the English-speaking artists picked up the imported technique and introduced the Canadian landscape to Abstract.

Nationalism among artists has been encouraged by the generosity of the Canadian government. Since 1957, the Canada Council has consistently granted artists money, so that many of them can live by their work. And one of the largest purchasers of Canadian art is Art Bank, a multi-million dollar fund which buys art for government offices.

French Canadian artists, for their part, have been influenced by their English-speaking counterparts and by the vastness of the Canadian landscape. But their basic concern is aesthetics rather than Canadianism, and French-speaking artists have achieved at least as much fame in other countries as in Canada.

The first important artist in Canada passed unnoticed. (Leduc (1864–1955) spent most of his life in a tiny village near Montreal. There in the late nineteenth century, he turned the light of French Impressionism on Canadian landscapes and still lifes. He produced one of the world's masterpieces, *Les trois pommes,* in 1887, though his works were hardly known until after his death.

One of his students was Paul-Émile Borduas (1905–60), who was the major influence on the development of Canadian art after the Group of Seven dissolved. And one of *his* followers, Jean-Paul Riopelle (born 1923), gave the world the technique of *tachisme,* or "action painting," in which each brushstroke has an importance of its own. French-speaking artists are fervent individualists, rather than self-conscious nationalists. But even so, they follow an artistic line of development which is unique to Canada.

The growth of art in Canada is fascinating. It is a dynamic (and evidently productive) conflict between English and French Canadians, between the nationalism of the English and the internationalism of the French, between the descriptive landscape and pure art. Yet insofar as its impact on the world is concerned, Canadian art has not yet really made a place for itself. That was left to Canadian architecture, which stunned visitors at Expo 67.

In the mid-1950s, an important new architectural movement evolved in Vancouver. There, because of the mild climate, architects designed houses that fit right into the environment. This movement's most important proponent is Arthur Erickson, who is greatly influenced by Japanese concepts. And his remarkable buildings seek both to express the environment and to impress the residents with the building.

Expo 67 introduced another architect to the world, Mose Safdie. Safdie's challenge was not *fitting into* an environment as it was in the mild West Coast, but *creating* an environment for city dwellers in the East. He designed a high density development to provide the maximum privacy and individuality possible and to economize on construction. The result was Habitat, 160 cube houses, stacked irregularly, so that each unit has its own roof garden.

One impressive accomplishment of Expo 67 was the re-planning of Montreal itself. A number of architects, artists, and planners contributed to the large shopping-office-motel complexes in the center of the city. Miles of underground streets, lined with elegant shops, branch out from these centers, protecting shoppers in winter. Montreal's subway, one of the cleanest, safest, quietest in the world, was completed in 1966. Writes Vancouver's Erickson, "Montreal emerged with a general better level of good buildings than perhaps any other city in North America." Many of Montreal's stone buildings date back to the seventeenth and eighteenth centuries, and before re-planning, the city had a solemn, ponderous air. By the time foreign visitors arrived for Expo 67, Montreal was no longer a quaint city but a modern one, with light and air as well as solemnity.

Good architecture in Canada has a distinctly Canadian flavor, which the large glass and steel skyscrapers (of which Canada has its share) lack. The new designs are assuming a passion for Canadian land and building materials. In fact, one daring church— Paroisse du Précieux Sang in St. Boniface, Manitoba (designed by Étienne Gaboury, and built in 1967)—looks suspiciously like a wigwam.

Canadian art and architecture came into their own in their own good time. They have developed at a natural pace with Canada. This has not been true of fiction. Because of the language barrier, there has not been the dynamic crossover found in painting; in literature, the two Canadas are strictly separated.

Yet even so, they both are uniquely Canadian: the French Canadians are interested in experimental fiction and draw their individual inspirations from literature outside Canada; the English Canadians are more interested in expressing "Canada."

Just as in painting before the twentieth century the most in-

teresting work is not by "artists" but by "illustrator
Canadian literature before the twentieth century w
tive" rather than "literary": the record of Champlain ᵃ ᵃ
colony by an historian named Lescarbot; the marvelous tales of
the early missionaries in *Jesuit Relations;* a journal published as
The Backwoods of Canada, kept by a genteel Englishwoman
named Catherine Parr Traill, who was abruptly thrown into the
role of wilderness immigrant.*

During the nineteenth century, when Canada was trying to
find itself in painting, literature had a parallel challenge: how to
put the Canadian environment down on paper. What style? What
words?

Among English Canadians, the novel developed in three
stages: the regional novel, the cosmopolitan novel, the Great Canadian Novel.

Regional novelists were the first to try to cope with the Canadian environment. Some of these writers have produced minor
masterpieces: the Plains are beautifully captured by Frederick Phi-
lip Grove and Sinclair Ross; British Columbia boasts Ethel Wilson; and from the Maritimes come Ernest Buckler and Hugh
MacLennan.

MacLennan's best novel, for instance, is *Barometer Rising,*
based on the great Halifax explosion of 1917. The harbor at Halifax was a floating powder keg during World War I. Inevitably two
ships collided, and one loaded with TNT caught fire. The sub-
sequent explosion sent particles over a mile into the sky, was
heard a hundred miles away, and killed 2,000 people. Out of this
catastrophe, MacLennan has woven a fascinating tale.

The "cosmopolitan" novel depends partly upon the peculiar
circumstances of Canadian publishing. Eighty-three percent of the
books sold in Canada are primarily published in foreign countries,
principally in the United States. By the early 1900s, when the

---

* Whole chapters could be devoted to Canadian histories and poetry. Discussion in this book,
however, is limited to fiction.

regional writers of Canada began making their mark, the United States was already mass-producing books. These ranged all the way from dime novels to European translations. U.S. books flooded the Canadian market. The exchange was not mutual. In order to sell in the United States, Canadian writers had to publish with a U.S. house. For those with enough drive or talent to make it to the top, it was much more convenient to move to the United States. This limited English Canadian literature to regional themes for nearly half a century.

Yet talent will out. And several writers so succeeded on an international level that they stunned even Canada: Robertson Davies, who writes about Catholic saints and stage magicians; Mordecai Richler, who writes about Montreal Jews; and Canada's master novelist, Morley Callaghan, who is preoccupied with the heroes that society builds up and then destroys.

Most of these writers have made their careers elsewhere than Canada. Richler is now a judge of the Book-of-the-Month Club in the United States; Callaghan was a colleague of Hemingway and Fitzgerald long before he became a best-selling author in his own country.

French Canadian literature, meanwhile, was not much affected by the United States where, after all, not many French-language books are printed. Furthermore, French Canadian publishers could sell their books directly in France, without having to associate themselves with French publishers. French Canada's great obstacle to a healthy literary development was due, not to U.S. encroachment, but to the internal structure of Quebec society.

The Conquest left some very wealthy French Canadians who "spoke" for their people, and many very poor Québécois. Right up through the 1950s, people in the latter class seldom received more than an elementary education. They were too poor; they had little time or money for education. In sharp contrast to this were the precious few wealthy Québécois, who received a classic education and were introduced to the arts and the languages. These were the ones who wrote.

No elite can long maintain a healthy art without fresh blood. Many of the *Canadien* works until recently were pale, fretful, and ingrown. This literary tradition produced only one fiction writer of real brilliance: Anne Hébert, whose novel *Kamouraska* (1970) was six months on the best-seller list and made a very successful movie.

The spell of caste was broken in the 1940s. Gabrielle Roy, a French Canadian from Manitoba, startled Canada with *Bonheur d'occasion* (published in the United States as *The Tin Flute*). It takes place entirely within the social framework of a working class district of Montreal: a large family living in the slum, a father who cannot find work, a mother who lives from one daily crisis to another, an ambitious daughter who is determined to raise herself out of this stew and find some security. Though the book is flawed toward the end by preachiness and false patriotism (it was published during World War II), it breached the stiff restrictions of Quebec society.

Today, the best *Canadien* fiction is "experimental." The most daring works of recent *Canadien* literature are by two brilliant young novelists, Marie-Claire Blais and Roch Carrier.

Blais made her debut in 1960 with *La belle bête* (translated into English as *Mad Shadows*). The characters in the story include a beautiful, vain woman, her retarded son who is inconceivably handsome, and her daughter who is ugly. The novel opens with the mother doting on the son and abusing her daughter. It is all downhill from there. The daughter pushes her brother's face into boiling water, destroying his beauty. The mother develops cancer of the cheek and dies hideously. As for the daughter, it is not her face that is destroyed, but her heart. What thoroughly astonished Quebec was that Blais was only twenty years old. How could such a young woman, the Québécois asked, write of such depravity? Critics were sure *La belle bête* was a one-time accident. Yet Blais has continued to produce volume after volume of strong and realistic fiction.

A more charming depravity is present in the works of Roch Carrier. *Floralie, où est tu?* (*Floralie, 'Where Are You?*) is a gripping novel about two people who have just been married. Young and loving, they leave the bride's village in the late afternoon, hoping to reach the groom's village before night. In the course of the journey, the young man pulls his bride from the buggy to make love in the forest. He discovers she is not a virgin and, this being Catholic French Canada, he beats her, rapes her, and leaves her. And so for the night, Anthyme and Floralie are separated. He finds that his horse and buggy have been stolen and starts the long trek to his village. She starts walking also, but is soon picked up, first by an Indian mystic and his pack of children, then by a troop of actors. Lost in the dark of the forest, alone and frightened, Anthyme begins to care less about virginity and more about Floralie. Slowly their paths once again lead them together.

The English Canadians, in the meantime, have gone on to what might be called the Great Canadian Novel. Nationalism has always been a preoccupation of English-speaking artists in Canada, and defining the totality of the Canadian land has been as much a problem for writers as for painters. English-speaking writers feel challenged to produce the novel that will represent "all of Canada." Good regional writers such as Hugh MacLennan have been seduced into trying their hands at the feat and have failed. Some fine authors, such as Margaret Atwood, who writes so poignantly about the situation of women, have allowed themselves to indulge in cheap anti-United States stereotypes in order to appear "Canadian." One competent novelist, Harry J. Boyle, even entitled his book *The Great Canadian Novel*—but it was not. And until recently, it seemed that no one was capable of capturing the total Canadian environment on paper.

Then in 1975, Margaret Laurence published *The Diviners*. The central character is the step-daughter of the town garbage collector, a wise old fool of a Scot. She works her way into college and is determined to have a successful career, but her ambitions are cut short when she marries a paternal college professor. She tolerates the restrictive marriage for a couple of years, eventually finding her own identity in writing. As her marriage is breaking up, she meets a man from her hometown, half-Cree, half-French, a Méti. He is a small-time singer who wanders from town to town. She becomes pregnant by him and decides to raise her daughter alone out in the country and live by her writing.

It is an ambitious novel, covering the country from eastern Canada to the Plains to the Pacific Coast, from the Old Scots culture to the Métis, from city to wilderness, from university to garbage dump. It is now being used in the schools of Ontario (although the town of Peterborough refused to use it on the basis that it contains "sex"), and it may be the closest anyone has come to writing "the great Canadian novel."

CULTURE FOR ALL

FOURTEEN

It may well be that the conventional arts, such as painting and fiction, cannot express the totality of Canada. Certainly the French Canadian artists show little interest in the notion of nationality, even in terms of French Canada. They manage to produce one or two political works during times of intense *Canadien* nationalism, but the impulse is weak. One can always sense the French Canadian, no matter how politically committed, glancing out the window of Quebec, eagerly awaiting the next international bombshell.

As for the English Canadians, who have taken on the burden of establishing a "national" culture or identity, the scanty results seem hardly worth the scrupulous struggle. The Group of Seven ended up as a shelter for mediocre talent. In literature, the closest the English Canadians have come to a "national" novel is Laurence's *The Diviners*—and for all Laurence's talent and craft, that book lacks the integrity and focus of a "great" novel. There was literally too much ground to cover.

The performing arts had scarcely taken root in Canada until the 1960s. There were exceptions. Winnipeg had a fine ballet company, and the National Ballet of Canada in Toronto also showed promise. In Quebec, where the provincial government has a long and unique history of government support to the arts, Montreal offered some performing arts—though little of it was fresh or lively. And very-British southern Ontario (with not only a town named London, but a river named Thames) nurtured a Shakespeare festival. Started by Tyrone Guthrie and Tom Patterson in 1953, the Stratford, Ontario, Shakespeare Festival is considered by some to be the best Shakespeare festival in the world. The Winnipeg Ballet Company, the Stratford Shakespeare Festival— these were all Canada could boast of until the 1960s.

Here again, the United States had pre-empted the action. If dancers, actors, and musicians wanted to work, they migrated south or, in some cases, to Europe. Canadian actors such as Lorne Greene and Raymond Burr made their acting careers in the United States, as did Canadian singers and songwriters such as Paul Anka and Leonard Cohen. And Actors Equity in New York had a virtual monopoly on organizing professional actors in Canada.

The same situation existed in television: most of the shows seen by Canadian viewers originated south of the border. The largest magazine distributions in Canada were held by *Time* and *Reader's Digest*. The feature film industry was non-existent because U.S.-based Famous Players movie houses, which monopolized the Canadian distribution, showed only Hollywood movies.

Just since the 1960s, practically overnight, this situation has been stood on its head. The Canadian government focused on Canadian culture and put its fullest possible powers into changing the situation. There are few governments that could overcome all obstacles and make such a dramatic change. But its precedent lay in government involvement with culture, in terms of "national" priorities, that went back nearly thirty years.

Communications, in a country where the regions are so separate, came first. In the 1930s, Canada established two important institutions, the Canadian Broadcasting Corporation and the National Film Board of Canada. The first was to encourage and control radio (and later television), which was vitally important to Canada with all its outlying areas. The second was to explore the then-new field of documentary film.

In 1951, the Massey Report focused the government's attention on the universities, and it began to pour money into educating its young. In the mid-1950s, and also as a consequence of the Massey Report, the Canada Council was established. This began to "seed" the culture with money to individual artists, local groups, and national agencies.

In the 1960s, with the burst of nationalism, both Canadian and *Canadien,* the government was once again stirred. This time it outlined a total cultural policy. Rather than concentrate arts in a few large Canadian cities, it decided to "de-centralize" them. A number of new museums were encouraged in towns that had none, and groups of performing artists were sponsored to travel all over the country.

The "seeds" are beginning to sprout. The National Ballet of Canada has filled out and now vies with the Winnipeg for national attention. Its last tour in the United States was greeted by critical raves. Les Feux Follets, the folk dancing ballet from Montreal, is one of the best folk groups in the world. And there are good theaters in Calgary, Charlottetown, Edmonton, Halifax, Montreal, Vancouver, and Winnipeg. In the late 1960s, the Vancouver Playhouse received international attention by commissioning "The Ecstasy of Rita Joe" by George Ryga, about the destruction of a young Indian woman. And even the distinguished Shakespeare Festival at Stratford has a competitor: the Shaw Festival. This began as a group of amateurs performing in a courthouse in Niagara-on-the-Lake. Now it has a fine theater designed by Ron Thom, and offers workshops in dance, opera, music, and drama.

In the early 1970s, Canada declared its independence from United States culture. It forced Canadian television and radio stations to use a majority of Canadian material in their programming. It cut government incentives to *Time* and *Reader's Digest*. It bullied Famous Players movie houses into showing Canadian films.

The most stunning results of these new policies have been in popular music. Canadian singers and musicians such as The Guess Who, Anne Murray, Gordon Lightfoot, Ian and Sylvia, Bachman-Turner Overdrive, and Joni Mitchell not only have topped Canadian charts for the first time, but also have become stars in the U.S. and England.

In other areas, too, the new government regulations are beginning to have an effect. Feature film, though still young, is beginning to develop in Canada. New magazines are springing up, and old ones have new life.

Government agencies established during the 1930s now have had enough time and money to mature. The combination of this healthy activity in communications, and the lack of activity in conventional arts, concentrated an unusual amount of artistic energy in technological fields. And communications, a thing of technology, became an art.

The lack of a feature film industry and theater channeled promising young playwrights into radio drama. The quality of radio plays is remarkably high, and a great number of them could be called "art." But it was the National Film Board that proved most dynamic. Now, if there is such a thing as "national art" in Canada, it is best represented by the National Film Board.

The NFB owns the largest documentary film studio in the

world, and is a leader in animation. It wins an average of seventy international film prizes each year for the two types of film. The NFB is divided into two sectors, French-speaking and English-speaking, with the French-language films comprising about a third of the total production. Here NFB replicates the pattern of Canadian art in general: the English-speaking sector is more likely to boost the practical wilderness documentary, while the French-speaking are more likely to be interested in the "pure art" of animation. There are many crossovers, of course, but it is a general pattern.

Not all the products of the gigantic NFB are "art." It makes a number of films for government agencies and departments, which are like bureaucratic mush the whole world over. These tend to pat the officials involved on the back rather than to give the viewer information. But the mush supports the good stuff, and the NFB has a lot of good stuff.

One of the best films is *City of Gold,* narrated by Pierre Berton. Berton is one of the best known writers and television personalities in Canada. He traced the history of the Canadian Pacific Railway in *The National Dream* and *The Last Spike.* His hometown is Dawson City, and the NFB asked him to narrate its proposed film about the Klondike gold rush. Mostly working from old photographs, Berton picked out just the right details to dramatize the gold rush. We see the endless line of would-be miners going over the Chikloot Pass. The Mounties, we are told, would not let them into the Yukon unless each one had a ton of provisions. The miners had to carry these goods, a hundred pounds at a time, over the steep, icy pass. They moved in a continuous line for nearly two years. And for all the gold fever, Berton points out, there was no murder or major theft throughout Dawson's boom. The film is studded with one such detail after another, painless history at its best.

Another fine film is *Death of a Legend,* about wolves. Canadians tend to identify with the wolf. One of Canada's (and the

world's) best nature writers, Farley Mowat, is famous for the classic *Never Cry Wolf,* in which he claims that wolves are not cun-
ning and ferocious but intelligent and relatively good-willed. *Death
of a Legend* picks up where Mowat left off. In what must be some
of the best footage in history, director Bill Mason follows a pack
of wild timber wolves through their seasons. The film shows the
pack of huge magnificent animals bringing down their prey, tear-
ing savagely at the meat. It shows them mating, and it shows—
incredibly—the little wolves being born inside the den. In one
breathtaking incident a lone wolf miraculously eludes a bounty
hunter in a snowmobile. The contrast between that handsome,
frightened beast and the bounty hunter who cannot even shoot
straight is enough to shame us.

Some NFB filmmakers make something of even the bureaucratic mush. One of the most perplexing films at first glance is
Change in the Maritimes, concerning a government prepared to
move Maritimers from their small fishing villages into the cities
where they could work in factories.

The stiff official in charge of centralizing the Maritimers
comes on the screen to explain why this program is necessary:
many Maritimers are seasonally unemployed, and most Maritimers are removed from the advantages of hospitals, welfare offices, etc. We are shown what he has in mind: modern Maritimers
sit in long factory rows assembling electrical equipment.

In between the official speeches are shots of another man outside his house in the Maritimes, repairing his boat. His face,
slightly lined by the weather, is healthy and relaxed. This, we
know, is a happy man. Why leave? he is saying. Sure, he doesn't
make much money, but he and his family get along well enough.
He has independence and dignity.

The outlooks of the two men, the official and the fisher, are
so different that at first one thinks the film is awkward. Then we
begin to see the filmmaker Robert Spry is playing one off against
the other. The official makes one last point: if stubborn old men

are still able to chop wood, let them stay behind; the rest of the Maritimers must move into the modern age. But the fisher in the prime of life gets the last word: "If you have a good thing, why leave it?"

The animation of the NFB does not lend itself as neatly to verbal description as documentary does. It is highly visual with little story line. Very few of the cartoons have dialogue: little blips of sound (not distinguishable as words, but perfectly clear in meaning) are used instead. Some of the best cartoons are *Wind*, about a delighted child's first discovery of wind; *Evolution*, a jazzy number with fantastic beasts gradually making their way from sea to land; and *Balablok*, a peace film in which balls and blocks do battle and are all changed by warfare into hexagons. The latter, which originated in the French-speaking sector of the NFB, took first prize at Cannes in 1974. These cartoons give us some idea of recurring themes in NFB animation.

The National Film Board of Canada received its basic ideas and perspectives from two men who were extraordinary in very different ways. John Grierson (1898–1972) came from a family of Scots lighthouse keepers. The son of a schoolteacher and a feminist, he grew up in Glasgow in the early 1900s. Glasgow at that time was a heavily industrialized city with appalling slums, and young Grierson became a radical. At the age of seventeen, he was blacklisted in Scotland and could find no work.

He moved to England and began working with the then-new medium of film. He was influenced by the muckraking journalism of Walter Lippmann in the United States, and by the films of Sergei Eisenstein when U.S.S.R. filmmaking was at its peak. Grierson saw in Eisenstein the vast sweep of history, "the movement of great masses" of people. Lippmann and Eisenstein brought Grierson's ideas into focus. He was also influenced by Canadian-educated Robert Flaherty, who was then making an as-yet-unnamed type of film about real people in real situations.

In 1929, Grierson made *Drifters*. Following the herring fishers of the North Sea, the film was the first British film to bring working people onto the screen as anything but comic relief. These were not humorous maids and butlers, but real people. It was so revolutionary that his producers demanded he cut the close-up shots of fishers' faces—as though a laborer's face were obscene or terrifying. To this new kind of film, Grierson gave the name "documentary."

This was the man whom the Canadian government brought to Canada in 1938 to head its new National Film Board, established in 1939. By one of those strange accidents of human sympathy, the colorless, conservative Mackenzie King and the vibrant, leftist Grierson hit it off immediately and remained loyal to one another for many years. Grierson was called "the Boss," "the Chief," and even "the Holy Terror." A hard drinker and a hard worker, he formed the NFB and bullied it to accomplishment far beyond what anyone had expected, determined to "interpret Canada to the Canadians." A strong Canadian nationalist, he sent his filmmakers to every corner of Canada.

Grierson had little patience with art. He seemed to feel that "art" was an excuse for laziness, self-indulgence, and vanity. The point was to be a good filmmaker. If a young filmmaker dared to point out that, after all, Grierson did employ *one* artist, Grierson would snap, "I can only afford *one* artist!" That artist was Norman McLaren. It is the paradox of Grierson that he was so scornful of artistic pretensions, and yet he gave young McLaren every freedom, all the room and support he needed, for his art.

McLaren also hails from Glasgow, but he is as different from Grierson as one could imagine. Grierson's eyes were piercing, demanding, combative. McLaren's eyes do not care: they are self-contained, watchful, distant. Grierson had the soul of an English Canadian. He wanted to build a national, democratic medium.

McLaren, despite his Scots origins, has the soul of a French Canadian. He is more interested in the latest artistic breakthrough than in the Canadian landscape.

McLaren immigrated from Glasgow to New York, where he developed the art of animation. Unlike Disney animation, which relies on characters and on a strong story line, McLaren animation relies on changing: an object or person is transformed magically into something else. And instead of photographing celluloid drawings, as is conventional, McLaren draws his images directly on the film. Nor does he use conventional sound. In some cases, he draws sound directly on the sound track; in others, he uses music. He never uses speech.

Grierson, who claimed to despise art, knew a genius when he saw one. In 1941, he invited McLaren to Canada. The practical documentary, he felt, would be balanced by McLaren's "bag of tricks." One of McLaren's first successes at the NFB was *Hen Hop,* in which a hen dances across the screen to the tune of a fiddle. A more recent film, *Spheres,* is a pure abstract, with pearl-like spheres colliding, blending, and multiplying in perfect symmetry.

In McLaren's career, every film counts. He has no interest in repeating himself or anyone else. Each film must be fresh and new; each must represent a technical challenge. Later artists, particularly among the French Canadians in the NFB, have picked up McLaren's techniques and developed them. McLaren's concept of change rather than character is evident in most of the award-winning cartoons. And most have "international" sound rather than identifiable language.

In addition to straight animation, McLaren has worked with filming people. While animation artists will cull his "pure" ideas for years to come, McLaren himself is best known to the general public for his films involving human beings. In *Neighbors,* which was inspired by Canada's controversial contribution to the Korean War, McLaren presents a classic story of greed—two men fight over a flower. They end up destroying each other's homes and families, and finally themselves. McLaren brought the techniques of animation to this film. Each frame is shot separately, so that the action is incredibly fast, and the men seem to fly through the air. The film, less than ten minutes long, is exhausting.

Pas de Deux is considered McLaren's masterpiece. In this film a lone dancer, a woman, is fascinated by her own mirror image. Then another dancer, a man, enters the frame. The dancers seem to sprout wings (made out of catching their past movements on camera); they blend into one another; they separate into different images. It is a beautiful, lyrical film, and it shows a deeply emotional side of McLaren.

Grierson was not encouraged to stay on in Canada after the late 1940s. His old supporter Mackenzie King died in 1950, and the 1950s were not kind to anyone with a radical background. He came back to Canada in 1964 for the twenty-fifth anniversary of the NFB. It was safe to ask him back: he was a has-been. Or so it was thought.

Surprisingly, he accepted a teaching post at McGill University. He had arrived just in time for the social turmoil and student unrest of the 1960s, and there in Montreal he was right in the thick of it. His classes started out with a handful of students; soon he was lecturing to 800 at a time.

After his death in 1972, the NFB made a film honoring its creator. Consisting of interviews with people who had worked with him, *Grierson* took a Bronze Reel at San Francisco in 1973. Another film covers McLaren. Called *The Eye Hears, the Ear Sees,* it consists of interviews with McLaren and film clips of most of his works. Much of the preceding account of Grierson and McLaren was drawn from these two films.

Seen together, the films begin to make sense of the fiery Grierson and the shy McLaren. They are not as different as they seem on the surface. McLaren's sensitivity to his material is an emotional relationship, and in his "people" films, there is a feeling for human beings that is as profound as Grierson's. We come to see him, not as cold and impersonal, but as deeply passionate. And Grierson, the adversary of ''art,'' might well have been an artist himself. He was one of those larger-than-life people who make art of everything they touch, whether it be a practical documentary, or an exchange of words, or even a government agency.

CANADA'S CENTURY

FIFTEEN

When Laurier became Prime Minister in 1896, he declared that the twentieth century would be Canada's century. With the increasing depletion of natural resources, no doubt many foreigners who look longingly at Canada's vast stretches of land agree with Laurier's prediction. Surely Canada will be the favored nation of the twentieth century. Perhaps it will be. But we shall not know until close to the end. The resources are there, sometimes in bountiful quantities. The problem is getting them out.

The discovery of the Athabaska Tar Sands in Alberta caused a sensation. The gummy black sands were mostly petroleum, in which there was more oil available than could be recovered (by con-

ventional methods) from all the rest of the world. The euphoria
soured when developers found that only a fraction of this enticing
oil could be extracted. The technology for fully exploiting the
sands does not yet exist.

Nor are the resources of Canada boundless. There is an estimated fifty trillion feet of natural gas that can be recovered from
Canada. It is being taken out at a rate of two trillion feet a year. In
another two decades, it will be gone. The same is true of the oil
reserves. Few people realize that Canada must import oil from
Venezuela; it does not produce enough to take care of its own
needs. Finds in the Arctic have been disappointingly small and expensive to extract. And Canada is pessimistic about finding new
reserves.

Nor is the great Boreal Forest an endless reserve for the pulp
and paper industries. Lumbering companies can now strip one
hundred square miles in a single week. And trees do not grow on
money; it takes a long time to re-forest an area that has been
stripped.

The situation with water is a little more promising, for Canada contains 25 percent of the world supply of fresh water. It is a
major producer of hydroelectric power and has built some of the
largest dams in the world. Yet even here the scale of research, exploration, development, and transportation is huge. The costs are
staggering.

Now under pressure to tap its resources, as those in the rest
of the world are depleted, the Canadian government is beginning
to measure its future. Because the necessary research is on such a
large scale, Canada has had to join with United States investors to
develop many of its resources. No Canadian company can compete with the big U.S. corporations. In addition, business interests
in Canada, often on a provincial level, have been tempted by fast
profits to bring in their U.S. counterparts as partners. As a result,
most of the resources and profits are ending up in United States
hands.

This has also led to foolish depletion. To develop the Athabaska Tar Sands while technology is still inefficient creates a terrible waste and rapidly uses up the sands while failing to get out most of what is in them. Now the Canadian government is beginning to slow this trend. Canada is not pinched for oil or gas yet, it chides the provinces; it can afford to wait for technology to catch up with its needs. Technology will be developed eventually.

Canada has backed away rather sharply from the United States during the last decade. The business community in Toronto (unlike the provincial interests) would like to see the profits from all these resources stay in Canada—and preferably in Toronto. The strongest impulse for nationalism and centralization has always come from this part of Canada. This, combined with Canada's increased stature in the world economy, and with the general wave of nationalist feeling during the 1960s, led Canada to adopt what it calls the Third Option.

The First and Second Options were to maintain the status quo and to move closer to the United States, respectively. The Third Option was to diversify Canada's economic relations. Instead of depending so heavily on the United States, Canada decided to reach out to other countries in the world, particularly Japan and European nations. Canada has succeeded in attracting a significant amount of Japanese capital, and has even considered joining the European Common Market.

One of its most significant moves was to establish the Canadian Development Corporation (CDC), with the intention of buying out some of the U.S. companies involved in Canadian industry. Another tremor was felt when the government expropriated a huge estate in Nova Scotia, which was owned by a woman in the United States. Canada is, in effect, declaring its independence from the United States—which is probably a healthy move for everyone concerned.

This is as delicate as independence from Britain was at the turn of the century. The United States is large, powerful, and very involved in Canada. Canada has no desire to offend its neighbor. Trudeau, like his political forebear Laurier, has managed to take a firm and graceful line.

The United States, for its part, was beginning to have difficulties with the Arab oil-producing nations at this time; it had no desire to offend its resource-rich neighbor to the north. And so far there has been no serious negative reaction from the United States to Canada's new stand. There has been grumbling. And when the CDC bought out Texas Gulf shareholders, that company filed suit. But the case was heard in U.S. courts, and Texas Gulf lost.

This withdrawal, as it was with Britain in the early 1900s, was touched off by U.S. military policy. Canadians have never felt comfortable with United States foreign policy. With NORAD, which has missile and radar lines across the Arctic, Canada has insisted on an indefinite treaty (which either nation can cancel at any time), and on the Canadian NORAD bases being manned by Canadians.

Another situation which might have caused bad feelings between the U.S. and Canada involved the U.S. draft resisters who fled to Canada during the Vietnam War. The United States government pressed Canada to send the fugitives home to be "punished." Canada hesitated, stalled, and finally took the stand that, since Canada had no draft of its own, there were no grounds for extradition. Most of the young men have been absorbed into the mainstream by now, acquiring landed-immigrant status or taking up jobs in the cities.

Quebec has gone through a parallel transformation, for Canadian nationalism and *Canadien* nationalism have always gone hand-in-hand. Quebec adopted a sort of Third Option, too, deciding to work toward independence from Canada. It, too, chose to diversify and develop stronger ties with other countries. Economically, the Quebec provincial government has stimulated several large-scale hydroelectric projects.

Quebec still has many problems, such as an unemployment

rate which persistently exceeds 10 percent. It tends to blame these problems on economic domination by Ontario, and this has led to the question of political as well as cultural independence from the rest of Canada.

During the 1970s, for instance, the Liberal government of the province began establishing cultural "delegations" in Paris, London, Brussels, Milan, and Dakar. These actually amounted to embassies, or perhaps semi-embassies, through which Quebec could deal with the outside world on its own.

Then on November 15, 1976, in one of the most startling elections in Quebec's history, René Lévesque of the *Parti Québécois* (PQ) was elected premier. A provincial minister during the "Quiet Revolution" of the 1960s, Lévesque had broken with the traditional political parties of Quebec to form the PQ. The PQ is committed to Quebec as a nation separate from Canada.

The PQ's main point is that Quebec's economy serves only to enrich the financial interests of Toronto, and that this cannot be changed without Quebec's becoming a completely separate political entity. Most English-speaking Canadians, on the other hand, are very disturbed by this proposed course of action. They feel that, while Quebec is generally justified in wanting to control its own education and culture, economic and political separation would be disastrous for Canada as a whole.

The PQ's first test was passing Bill 101, which legislates that all students (except English-speaking children already living in Quebec) attend French-speaking schools. This applies to all immigrants, and to English-speaking children moving to Quebec from other provinces of Canada. But the *Parti*'s real test of strength will be over the question of separation. This has many opponents in Quebec as well as in the rest of Canada. But so far its effects have been basically positive, in that many English Canadians have become aware of Quebec's special economic and political problems.

Moreover, English Canada has been stimulated by Quebec's

radicalism to discover its own failings, needs, and remedies. Here, too, a principal concern is education. One very controversial subject in higher education is the "Americanization" of the universities. In many Canadian colleges, more than half the faculty are not Canadian-born, whereas in the United States only 2.5 percent of the academics are not United States-born. This, along with the popularity of U.S. magazines and television, tends to educate young people more in U.S. culture than in Canadian culture. One Laurentian University professor raised a stir when he discovered that the 260 term papers in his sociology course were virtually all on United States subjects. Now the pressure is on to hire more Canadians.

Higher education has developed considerably since the 1951 Massey Report recommended government aid to the universities. Now Canada boasts a number of good institutions, which have mushroomed dramatically in size and number. A new phenomenon during the 1960s and 1970s is the growth of "post-secondary" schools, which offer higher education at a more modest level than the universities, much like community colleges and trade schools in the U.S. A university education in Canada is a good deal less expensive than in the United States, but still too costly or impractical for many students. And this new type of school fills a great need.

Only three-fourths of the young people in Canada graduate from high school. And this is not likely to change. The percentage of students graduating in 1970–71 was 73.2; in 1974–75, it was 74.5. The projection by Statistics Canada for 1984–85 is 76.9 percent. Why?

In Newfoundland and the Maritimes, many young people must start work early in order to help out their families. In Quebec, where 40 percent drop out, young people must cope, not only with the poverty, but also with the second-class status of French Canadians which deprives a young person of motivation. It becomes easier and more attractive to "hang out" on the street than to attend classes which will not change one's economic place in life.

And there is another phenomenon in Canada which accounts for a fair number of drop-outs, especially among the young men. Canadians tend to place more emphasis on having a job and being self-sufficient than do people in the United States. Because of the seasonal nature of much Canadian work and large-scale projects such as the Athabaska Tar Sands, many youths leave home to travel about the country, earning good wages and living hard. It is common to meet a young man of seventeen or eighteen on one of the trains, traveling coach class with a "micky" of whisky in his pack (the drinking age is eighteen in Canada), going someplace where there is a job waiting.

This is not the same as the "hippie" phenomenon of the 1960s in the United States. The trips young Canadians take are not to Mecca but to a job, and few if any are rebelling against society or parents. Some of them, in fact, go home to live with their families between jobs. Then once again, like the youthful *coureurs de bois* and with the blessings of father and mother, they "take to the wilds."

Yet among the young people who do graduate from high school, the number who go on to college has increased dramatically since the Massey Report. In 1955, only 65,000 were enrolled in college. In 1960, the number was 114,000, almost doubled. By 1967, it was 232,000. Likewise during the 1960s, the number of students in elementary and secondary schools increased by 50 percent, and the staff by 70 percent. All told, 30 percent of Canada's population is involved in education, in either learning or teaching.

These profound changes in Canadian society during the last decade are now beginning to come to the surface. In politics, this has taken the form of a new national party, a "third" party that has challenged the traditional Conservative and Liberal parties. Canada has always had more active political parties than the

United States, but nevertheless the rise of the New Democratic Party (NDP) is truly astonishing.

Or perhaps not, considering its history. Social democracy (on which the NDP is based) has always been a strong force in Canadian politics, one way or another. Though there was no official Social Democratic Party for forty years, from 1921 to 1961, the thread remained strong.

In 1921, in a burst of euphoria over the Russian Revolution, the Social Democratic Party voted itself into the Communist Party. When the Communist Party was legally suppressed in the 1930s, the militant impulse went two ways. The less radical farmers and intellectuals formed the liberal Co-operative Commonwealth Federation (CCF). The more radical populists turned to Social Credit (that odd combination of socialism and fascism) in the West, just as Quebec turned to the *Union Nationale* (the combination of *Canadien* nationalism and fascism) in the East. Both were quick to disassociate themselves from the embattled Communists.

The CCF carried the social-democratic thread through to the 1960s. Never a truly national party, it was nevertheless strong in agricultural Ontario and Manitoba, and it controlled the provincial government of Saskatchewan for thirty years.

The same thread was carried by urban labor. Most union leaders expelled the Communists when the government heat was on, turned their backs on social reform, and were content to quarrel with industry over the pie. Within the largest union affiliation, the Canadian Labour Congress (CLC), however, there remained many *social democrats,* who kept the thread of social reform alive and consistently urged the CLC to recognize the CCF as an official labor party. In 1961, the basically agricultural CCF and the basically urban CLC jointly launched a more militant party, the New Democratic Party.

In the early 1970s, the NDP made a dramatic entrance into national politics. It took the provincial governments in Manitoba and Saskatchewan—which, considering their CCF histories, is not surprising—and in British Columbia—which, considering its Social Credit history, is surprising indeed. The party is strong in Ontario, weak in the Maritimes and Quebec. The Maritimes have a deeply rooted U.E. Loyalist conservative history, and probably will not provide an immediate area for the NDP.

In Quebec the thread of social democracy was carried on by such political leaders as Thérèse Casgrain. But it never gained much strength under Duplessis, and of course the virulent anti-Communism of the Church steered Québécois away from any taint of social reform. Then came the "Quiet Revolution" of the 1960s and the formation of the *Parti Québécois* under Lévesque. The NDP, though it did not generally appeal to the French-speaking Québécois, helped the PQ in its rise to power.

No parties can change overnight the historical circumstances that limit development. French Quebec is limited economically. No matter how independent the Québécois are culturally and politically, the fact remains that the economy is controlled by *Anglais*—many of them from Toronto. The recent pressure of Quebec nationalism has led some companies, such as Air Canada, to relocate. And it has led the financial elite to use French Canadian figureheads for their projects. But this changes nothing: it is the English Canadian frequenters of the Windsor Hotel in Montreal, rather than the French Canadian officials at the Chateau Frontenac in Quebec City, who control the lifeblood of Quebec.

The Maritimes also have a long-time history of an economic elite, which can be traced back to their period of U.E. Loyalist domination. The tenor of politics is conservative, and most Maritimers do not really participate in the political process. Nova Scotia is primarily Scots, and in some backwoods areas, Gaelic is still spoken. British—both Scots and English—form the majority in New Brunswick, but there is a sizable minority of French Canadians. These last will probably be in the majority soon. Prince Edward Island is basically British. But Scots, U.E. Loyalists, and

Acadians alike are wedged into a rigid, outdated political system.

Because seasonal employment has always characterized the Maritimes, the average working person would be at the mercy of the system were it not for organization. Unions in the mines, steel plants, and railroads began early and violently, and are now fairly strong. The Maritime workers who are unionized are quite conscious of their "rights," and resist stubbornly any attempts to erode them. The loyalty of Maritimers to the worker leads to a certain amount of unofficial resistance. Many Maritimers, for instance, will not use postal codes on mail: it means one less job for someone like themselves.

In Newfoundland, as well as in parts of the Maritimes, the fisheries that always sustained the Atlantic peoples, even in the worst of years, are now in bad shape. During the last ten years, the huge, highly efficient boats from the U.S.S.R. and Japan have literally emptied the once-plentiful seas. The smaller fishers of Atlantic Canada, many of them individuals who spent years scraping together enough money to buy their own boats and equipment, are going under very quickly. In response, Canada has affirmed a 200-mile commercial limit, so that foreign ships can be kept away from the coasts. Whether this will be enforceable remains to be seen.

Poorer than the Newfoundlanders, and less sustained by their bits of land, are the Indians. It is all very well for the Canadian government to pat itself on the back for treating the Indians better than they were treated in the United States. The truth is that the reservation system is a shoddy, inadequate system at best, and that it destroys the Indians—with malnutrition, prostitution, alcoholism, and dependency. The average life expectancy of the Canadian Indian is under forty years. The Canadian government's responsibility for this can be summed up in the following sentence from the Indian Act of 1880: "The term person means an individual other than an Indian."

This concept still guides the Department of Indian Affairs. Journalist Heather Robertson points out in her book *Reservations Are for Indians* (1970) that Canadian Indians cannot sell the grain or livestock they raise themselves. That is done by Indian Affairs, which keeps the profits to spend as it sees fit. Because Indians make nothing if they work their own land, they rent it to white farmers for a pittance, or go on welfare. And Indians cannot make out a will without approval by the government. In life and death both, the Indian is government-owned.

Women have an additional outrage to bear, for their race is determined by the husband. If an Indian woman marries a non-Indian, she loses her Indian status and any of the treaty benefits that accompany it. Unable to return to the reservation, non-status Indians are among the poorest people in Canada.

It did not have to be this way. George Woodcock in *Canada and the Canadians* gives us another example. After reminding us that alcoholism is a social problem rather than a physiological one, he writes:

My experience suggests that in areas where Indians have been able to retain their self-respect, and the respect of other people in the local community, drunkenness is not a problem. I am thinking particularly of the Gitksan people of the Skeena River in northern British Columbia, whose country I have visited often. The region was penetrated late by the white men, and the Indians, who never signed a treaty, retained their independence to such a degree that even in the 1950s the people of the village of Kitwancool policed their boundaries to keep strangers away from their fishing and hunting grounds. For their part, the local white people have shown a respect for Indian traditions and for the arts of the Gitksan; a museum has been built in the local town of Hazelton to house a fine collection of artifacts assembled by the two peoples in co-operation. The relative harmony that characterizes racial relationships in the area extends even to the tavern of the local hotel, where Indians, whites and the local Chinese meet and mingle in perfect cordiality. As a consequence, in Hazelton one saw very little Indian drunkenness.

A good deal of militancy on the part of young Indians is beginning to squeeze some response from the government. And self-help projects have had small successes here and there.

Part of the answer is organization. Nova Scotia Indians, in particular, have developed several lines of action. Indians from the Pictou Landing reservation occupied, claimed, and won a small nearby island. Abenakis from the Millbrook reservation opened the Abenaki Motor Inn in 1975. The Eskasoni reservation is developing a solid area of community clam beds. And Eskasoni women are organizing non-status Indians to obtain equal rights for Indian women. The Union of Nova Scotia Indians provides a focus for the various reservations and bands, and publishes its own paper, *The Micmac News*. Whatever the solutions, it will be the Indians who find them, not the government.

Canadian feminists have reached the same conclusion in regard to women. But here the government seems more responsive. Canada was ahead of Britain and the United States in giving women the vote. It allowed women into some of the colleges, and it allowed married women to own property, even before the turn of the century.

But these facts are deceptive. As late as 1928, the Supreme Court ruled that women were not "persons." As late as 1955, no married woman could work for Canada's largest employer, the federal government. As late as 1972, of the 68,000 women employed by the federal government, only one held the rank of "senior executive."

Not counting homemakers, women comprise about a third of Canada's labor force, and on the average earn about half the wage of the average working man. In blue collar work, women are largely excluded from the well-paid construction jobs and from industries with strong unions. In white collar work, they are largely excluded from executive, professional, and technical jobs, particularly the well-paid ones.

Women have come a long way since the mid-1800s, when Canada's first Inspector General for Hospitals, Dr. James (Miranda) Barry, had to maintain a lifelong male disguise in order to practice medicine. They have come a long way since the early 1900s, when a premier of Manitoba would dare to say, "I don't want a hyena in petticoats talking politics to me. I want a sweet gentle creature to bring me my slippers." But they have not come far enough.

Feminism has a strong and interesting history in Canada, particularly on the Plains during the 1920s and 1930s. The new resurgence of the 1970s seems more evenly spread. Almost every province has its women's newspaper (there are at least two dozen in Canada), and every one has at least one "status of women" committee. Especially active centers are in Toronto, Montreal, and Vancouver. Progress with the government has been slow but fairly substantial. Of the 122 recommendations made by the Royal Commission on the Status of Women in 1970, about two-thirds have been implemented to some extent.

Canada will never run smoothly so long as large segments of its population are suppressed on the basis of race or sex. And it will never run smoothly so long as its provinces feel bound hand-and-foot to big business in eastern Canada. One of Canada's most dynamic economists, Kari Levitt of McGill University, questions the desirability of centralization and large-scale corporate development. "In the free enterprise system," she writes (in *Natural Resource Development in Canada,* 1973), "the only institutions that seriously engage in economic planning are the large corporations." It was industrialization, after all, that first stimulated nationalism. In one sense, industry *is* the national impulse, and everything that modifies this comes from the outside, from the provinces and peoples who refuse to be steamrolled. The tension between the nation and its regions has always existed. It is what has formed Canada.

One current conflict is between the federal government and Alberta. Oil-rich Alberta is feeling independent. There are several reasons for the conflict of interests, the most important being the division of the profits from Alberta's oil wells and Athabaska Tar Sands. The provinces own their own resources—which gives them a great deal of power. Once any resource crosses provincial or national boundaries, however, the federal government can assert some control. Albertans feel frustrated by the limitations set on their trade. But even more galling is the federal government's involvement with the Northwest Territories.

For a long time Edmonton, Alberta, the natural jumping-off point for the Arctic, has been the center of Northwest activity. Alberta even owns the major airline, Pacific Western, that services the little communities in the North. When it looked as though Arctic resources might be very valuable indeed, the federal government's interest in the Northwest Territories (NWT) picked up. It encouraged twenty-six companies, many of them from the United States, to form the Arctic Gas Consortium. Arctic Gas was to build a mammoth natural gas pipeline across the Northern Yukon and down the Mackenzie River Valley to the United States.

Neither Alberta nor the Northwest Territories liked the idea of a big U.S.-oriented organization moving in. From Alberta's point of view, it meant that much of the profits would bypass the province. The Northwest Territories knew that the huge impersonal Arctic Gas would not even hear their protests about ecological factors and Native rights. The final blow came when Arctic Gas moved its headquarters from Alberta to Toronto. The Northwest Territories harbors a traditional hatred for Toronto, feeling, and with justification, that Toronto historically has "used" the Territories with no consideration for its land and inhabitants.

Several alternatives have been suggested and commissions appointed to study them. But in general, Canadians from all the provinces have shown a great concern for both Native rights and the environment in the Northwest. Some Canadians feel that perhaps Canada does not need another gas line at all.

The federal government is now reaching out to claim its last great hinterland. As with Manitoba a century ago, it intends to claim the Northwest Territories without granting provincial status. The last thing the federal government needs is another fractious province; it wants a "colony." And as with Manitoba, it can do so only by running roughshod over the people who live there. It has a better chance of doing so in the Northwest Territories.

The Northwest Territories contains only 37,000 permanent residents, 17,000 of whom are Innuit. They were the last people to be touched by white civilization. The introduction of the gun rapidly depleted the caribou, and by the 1950s, many inland Innuit were starving to death. The federal government stepped in, first to help, then to "civilize." They established communities throughout the Arctic, to which the Innuit were sent, drawn, and urged. Like the Indians, they were soon dependent on welfare and alcohol to sustain them in those wretched hamlets.

Young women barely grown are sexually exploited by the white men who come to make "quick bucks" in the Arctic and to leave after a summer. As with the Indians, the children are transported far from their parents and housed in large government schools, or "hostels," where none of the staff speaks Innuit. As with the Indians, some of these children commit suicide. What kind of system would make an eight-year-old child so desperate as to commit suicide? It is the reservation system.

Life for these people does not have to be this way—but it is and it will be.

The Canadian government might have taken a leaf from the tale of the Indians and made the transition between the old way of life and the new more creative, more responsive to what the Innuit want, more dignified, less wasteful of a rare and generous people. But no impulse for change in policy will come from Ottawa. It has always taken outside pressure, the people themselves, to change the course of Canadian expansion.

Unfortunately, the Innuit are not even as organized as the Indians. They do not have tribes. There are *no* roads in the Arctic, and the little villages, spread over great distances, are isolated from one another year round. The only transportation or communication is by plane and radio. The nomadic Innuit never had any political organization. Worse, their property rights are not legally recognized. As far as the Canadian government is concerned, the Innuit do not have a territory, as do the Indians. There have been a few gallant attempts by younger Innuit to develop a group identity. One man in Inuvik, some 500 miles north of the Arctic Circle, runs an Innuit-language radio station and a newspaper named *The Drum*. But for the most part, the Innuit in settlements such as Inuvik just want to get drunk, and the whites there just want to get *out*.

A nation that does not account for all of its people cannot be considered successful. Canada's faults are no greater than those of any other major country in the world. Its problems are no larger. And Canada has a better chance of solving them than most. Because capital was slow in developing in Canada, the government financed large-scale projects. It now "owns," or partly "owns," the Canadian National Railroad, Air Canada, and a number of other public corporations. This gives the government tremendous leverage and flexibility when it does move toward positive solutions. Because of its unique form of government, Canada hesitates, weighs, stalls; it is slow and awkward. But once a decision is reached, as in the attempt to clean up the polluted Great Lakes, Canada does the job more quickly and more thoroughly than does the United States.

Most important, Canada is a young country. The development of its resources will require massive and unknown technol-

ogy, but Canadians know that that will come in time. They can afford to wait. Development in Canada has always lagged behind
that of the United States, and it has learned many lessons from the
experiences of its rash neighbor. While the U.S. was in the frying
pan, Canada was in the deep-freeze. Canada learned about ecological considerations before it was too late. It learned about Cold
War politics before it was too committed. For all of Canada's
anti-U.S. sentiments of the moment, it might very well thank the
United States for making painful mistakes in its stead. And if the
Canadian nation finds the way to accommodate all of its peoples,
the future looks bright—as bright as the midnight sun of an Arctic
summer.

FOR FURTHER READING

History

There are several multivolume histories of Canada. The most venerable is the colossal work of Francis Parkman, published by Little, Brown in Boston during the late nineteenth and early twentieth centuries. Less formidable but more modern and readable histories include:

Creighton, Donald. 3 vols: *The Empire of the St. Lawrence; The Road to Confederation; Canada's First Century*. Toronto: Macmillan, and New York: St. Martin's, 1956–70. Creighton has also written a fine two-volume biography of John A. Macdonald.

Lanctot, Gustave. *A History of Canada*. Trans. Josephine Hambleton and Margaret M. Cameron. 3 vols. Cambridge, Mass.: Harvard University Press, 1963–65. This is one of the few histories of Canada from a French Canadian viewpoint.

A number of good single-volume histories exist, but the best by far is:

Brebner, J. Bartlett. *Canada: A Modern History*. Ann Arbor: University of Michigan
   Press, 1960, and Toronto: Ambassador, 1960.

Two popular histories that are particularly compelling and colorful are:

Berton, Pierre. *The National Dream: The Great Railway 1871–1881*. Toronto: McClel-
   land and Stewart, 1970.
———. *The Last Spike: The Great Railway 1881–1885*. Toronto: McClelland and
   Stewart, 1971.
   Berton's two-volume history of Canada's intercontinental railroad is one of the
   most widely read works in Canada. A native of the Northwest Territories, Berton
   also has written agreeable books on the Klondike and Native Peoples.
Hill, Douglas Arthur. *The Opening of the Canadian West: Where Strong Men Gathered*.
   New York: John Day, 1967, and Don Mills, Ont.: Longman Canada, 1972.

Society

The following books are listed not only for their general analyses of institutions at
   international, national, and French Canadian levels, respectively, but also because of the disturbing issues they raise:

Levitt, Kari. *Silent Surrender: The Multinational Corporation in Canada*. Toronto:
   Macmillan, 1970.
Porter, John A. *The Vertical Mosaic: An Analysis of Social Class and Power in Canada*.
   Toronto: University of Toronto Press, 1965.
Vallieres, Pierre. *White Niggers of America: The Precocious Autobiography of a
   Quebec Terrorist*. Trans. Joan Pinkham. New York: Monthly Review Press,
   1971.

Observations

The United States' foremost man of letters and Canada's foremost man of letters have
   both been moved to record their wonderfully witty and lucid insights into the
   unique phenomenon of Canada:

231

Wilson, Edmund. *O Canada: An American's Notes on Canadian Culture*. New York: Farrar, Straus and Giroux, 1965.

Woodcock, George. *Canada and the Canadians*. Rev. ed. Harrisburg, Pa.: Stackpole Books, 1973.

The Land

Mowat, Farley. *Never Cry Wolf*. Boston: Little, Brown (Atlantic Monthly), 1963.
One of the best nature writers in the world, Mowat has also written books on the Native Peoples and the Arctic.

Warkentin, John, ed. *Canada: A Geographical Interpretation*. Toronto: Methuen, 1968.

Native Peoples

The last fifteen years have spawned an astonishing number of truly good books on the Native Peoples of North America—rightfully so, for the cultures of the first inhabitants of this continent are closely tied to issues of both environmentalism and human rights. The following are books that were particularly useful to me:

Driver, Harold E. *Indians of North America*. 2nd rev. ed. Chicago: University of Chicago Press, 1969.

Oswalt, Harold H. *Eskimos and Explorers*. Novato, Ca.: Chandler & Sharp Publishers, 1979. Oswalt has, so to speak, made Native Peoples his life, and has written extensively on the Innuit, or Eskimos. This book is particularly good in relating the Innuit to the Arctic environment.

Robertson, Heather. *Reservations Are for Indians*. Toronto: Lorimer, 1970. This is a strong and well-reasoned argument for Native rights.

Architecture

Ede, Carol Moore. *Canadian Architecture 1960/1970*. Intro. Arthur Erickson. Don Mills, Ont.: Burns and MacEachern, 1971.

Sadie, Moshe. *Beyond Habitat*. Cambridge, Mass.: M.I.T. Press, 1970, and Montreal: Tundra, 1970.

Literary Collections

Smith, A. J. M., ed. *The Oxford Book of Canadian Verse*. Toronto: Oxford University Press, 1960.

Richler, Mordecai, ed. *Canadian Writing Today*. Harmondsworth, Middlesex, Eng.: Penguin, 1970.

Weaver, Robert, ed. *Canadian Short Stories*. Toronto: Oxford University Press, 1966.

Weaver, Robert, ed. *Canadian Short Stories: Second Series*. Toronto: Oxford University Press, 1968.

Fiction

Canada produces so many fine novelists that there is not space to list them all. This list, therefore, is merely of a few of my particular favorites:

Atwood, Margaret. *Surfacing*. New York: Simon and Schuster, 1972.

Blais, Marie-Claire. *Mad Shadows (La belle bete)*. Trans. Merloyd Lawrence. Toronto: McClelland and Stewart, 1960.

Callaghan, Morley. *The Many Colored Coat*. Toronto: Macmillan, 1951, and New York: Coward-McCann, 1960.

Carrier, Roch. *Floralie, Where Are You? (Floralie, ou est-tu?)* Trans. Sheila Fischman. Toronto: Anansi, 1971.

Davies, Robertson. *Fifth Business*. New York: Viking, 1970.

Hebert, Anne. *Kamouraska*. Trans. Norman Shapiro. New York: Crown, 1973.

Laurence, Margaret. *The Diviners*. Toronto: McClelland and Stewart, 1974, and New York: Knopf, 1974.

MacLennan, Hugh. *Barometer Rising*. Toronto: McClelland and Stewart, 1958.

Richler, Mordecai. *The Apprenticeship of Duddy Kravitz*. Boston: Little, Brown, 1959.

Roy, Gabrielle. *The Tin Flute (Bonheur d'occasion)*. New York: Reynal & Hitchcock, 1947.

INDEX